JOSEPH CONRAD
AND HIS CHARACTERS

JOSEPH CONRAD

RICHARD CURLE

JOSEPH CONRAD
AND
HIS CHARACTERS

A STUDY OF SIX NOVELS

NEW YORK / RUSSELL & RUSSELL

TO

MY SISTER SYBIL

FIRST PUBLISHED IN 1957
COPYRIGHT © 1957, BY RICHARD CURLE
REISSUED, 1968, BY RUSSELL & RUSSELL
A DIVISION OF ATHENEUM HOUSE, INC.
BY ARRANGEMENT WITH WILLIAM HEINEMANN LTD., LONDON
L.C. CATALOG CARD NO : 68-10913
PRINTED IN THE UNITED STATES OF AMERICA

CONTENTS

CONTENTS

ACKNOWLEDGEMENTS

IT IS the Author's pleasant duty to make some acknowledgements. To the Trustees of the Conrad estate, to Messrs. J. M. Dent and Sons Ltd., publishers of the Collected Edition of Conrad's works, the twenty-one volumes of which are kept in print, and to Mr. E. F. Bozman, Editorial Director of the firm, I owe a very special debt of gratitude for their generous kindness in allowing me to quote freely from the novels I discuss. Without this permission my book would have been pointless, if not, indeed, impossible, and I cannot thank them sufficiently. I am also very grateful to Mr. Jocelyn Baines who, in the midst of his own labours on an elaborate study of Conrad, not only found time to read most of my manuscript, but gave me valuable ideas and essential facts in the most unstinting manner. Again, I am much indebted to Mr. Ivo Vidan of Yugoslavia, whose pamphlet, *One Source of Conrad's 'Nostromo'* (reprinted from *The Review of English Studies*, Vol. VII, No. 27), was kindly sent to me by him. It tells the remarkable story of the similarity of names between certain characters in G. F. Masterman's *Seven Eventful Years in Paraguay* (1867) and Conrad's South American masterpiece. And, of course, I am under obligation to some earlier writers about Conrad, both critical and biographical. I would like also to express my thanks to various friends, such as Miss Mary Morris, Miss Veronica Wedgwood, Mr. John Conrad and Mr. Frank Pitt, for the encouragement and interest they have shown. Finally, I wish to thank Mr. Jonathan Price of Messrs. Heinemann Ltd. for the skill and perspicacity with which he prepared my typescript for press.   R. C.

AUTHOR'S NOTE

When Conrad employs a row of dots in the middle or at the end of a sentence, which is not very frequently, I have placed three dots. When I employ them, which is more frequently, to show an omission in a quotation – short or long is of no consequence provided the idea be continuous – I have placed six dots.

PREFACE TO THE 1968 PRINTING

I WAS ENCOURAGED to write this book, a study of the chief characters of the six novels in Conrad's middle, and greatest, period, by the imminent approach of the centenary of his birth—Conrad was born on December 3rd, 1857—and the feeling I had that this event would lead to a special surge of interest in his work. I had thought over the subject for a long time, for it appeared to me that if I could only make people *see* these figures, the true nature of Conrad's psychological insight, enhanced by his superb art and interwoven with the fabric of the scene, would really emerge.

Whether my effort had much success I rather doubt, for of recent years there has sprung up an entirely new school of Conrad criticism, a very able school, but one inclined, as I believe, to miss, in its delving subtleties, the vital points of Conrad's supremacy. In so brief an introduction I can, alas, do no more than touch upon this matter, but I feel strongly that such brilliant expositions may positively blur the finer outlines of this tremendous creator.

Conrad once wrote to me that I was the man "who certainly knows my work best and no less certainly is known as my closest intimate, but before all is the best friend my work has ever had" (July 14th, 1923). And I cannot help wondering whether, knowing him and his writings as I do, I ought not to appreciate, better than most critics, how he visualised his characters. For an author's personality must impinge itself upon a reader, and a sympathy between their points of view must exist, if a comprehension of his work is to achieve any sort of depth.

All this, of course, has nothing to do with the sheer power of such a writer as Conrad, that insoluble mystery which is the crux of everything; but at least it may be a guide to his intentions and does draw one very close to his characters. Indeed, in their invincible reality they seem to step out of the pages to meet one.

It is not necessary here to quote Conrad on his own works, although I could do so from the words he wrote in my copies, for their matchless intensity lies not in the generalised summaries such notes usually suggest, but, needless to say, in how he developed his characters and breathed vitality into them. A book about books, just as an introduction to a book about books, is, after all, only a foretaste of the real thing, its purpose being, apart from glimpses of self-opinionated egotism, to induce the public to study the originals for themselves, and to offer them the potential thrill of making their own discoveries.

And how these figures crowd upon us, men and women in settings which become almost part of them, more actual than the people we meet, more touching or more terrible, more entrancing or more evil. They are all there, a whole world of animate figures, silently awaiting our judgement.

I am now very old and this will almost certainly be my last book on Conrad. What I would have wished, of course, is that my performances had equalled my intentions, but maybe in the mass of my Conradian writings, covering over fifty years—as long ago as 1932 a pamphlet showed sixty-six Conrad entries under my name—I may have had some influence in moulding the opinion in what I hold to be the right direction. Who can tell?

But though I may never again write at length about Conrad, he and his books are constantly in my mind. And especially, perhaps, as I grow older and older, his words, "all passes and all changes," which, with their noble melancholy and calm acceptance of time's ravages, always affect me profoundly. And yet, completely as I agree with this attitude, I am quite sure that, as long as I survive, nothing will pass or change in my ever-grateful memories of Joseph Conrad and my admiration for his inspired genius.

January, 1968   RICHARD CURLE

INTRODUCTION

I HAVE LONG WANTED to write such a book as this, for it
seems to me that Conrad was so consummate an artist, so pene-
trating a psychologist, and, above all, so profoundly creative
that his characters repay study almost more than those of any
other novelist. A novel is, in its very nature, selective, a chosen
segment of life, and there may be traits and subtleties in the
characters not observable at once and implications that transcend
the boundaries of the novel itself. Of course, one has to be careful
not to read into the characters more than the author intended,
but one should never forget that what an imaginative writer
says about his figures is not all he has envisaged, but only what
the narrative calls for.

So highly individualised a novelist as Conrad is sure to arouse
particularly personal opinions, and though this has its own
value, it can be a pitfall. For over-enthusiasm may be as
dangerous as instinctive antipathy, and the tendency to put
oneself into the minds of the characters may be as misleading
as the idea that sympathy or dislike can take the place of critical
judgment. Probably all criticism is biased to some degree, but
I have tried to obviate or lessen the charge of being too partisan
by the employment of ample quotations. Conrad had the gift
of making us *see* the people of whom he wrote, and though it is
likely enough that one could sometimes pick one's quotations
in such a manner as to maintain a special thesis, yet knowing
Conrad as well as I did, I hope I have interpreted—in most

cases, at any rate—his men and women as he himself meant them to be interpreted.

Perhaps no novelist, in the delineation of his characters, appears to follow invariably his original conception, for the course of the story can make demands on minute points of verisimilitude, and minor discrepancies can scarcely fail to creep in now and again; but it is true that when a reader thinks that a novelist has gone astray, it may only imply that he has not really understood the character and has been misled by his failure to appreciate what the author was doing. And with such a writer as Conrad, who worked with meticulous care and always kept his objective in view, it is unwise to assume that what may seem improbable in attitude or behaviour is necessarily improbable. After all, when we strike others as being least ourselves we still are ourselves, and in the stress of emotion anything, within certain limits, is possible.

And it may be that, in Conrad's case, such divergencies or misapprehensions are partly due to the fact that he based some, at least, of his characters on people he had met or seen or heard of. Thus it may occasionally happen that we cannot keep pace with the sequence of the impulse because, through his own detailed knowledge, concentrated in the ardour of his creation, Conrad knew so much more than he could put on paper that there is, as one might say, a sort of elision of memory in which he takes for granted more than the reader can clearly decipher. (I am not sure, however, whether this point arises in the six novels here considered.) Conrad told me that he had no aptitude for invention – he was talking explicitly of his plots, but he may have intended to include his characters – and though such a remark is very deceptive in that from the merest skeleton he could construct an elaborate edifice, yet it may account both for the intensity of his vision and for intermittent obscurities. It is not a matter of any importance, for his figures are rounded out with extraordinary fullness and, anyhow, to feel their inner truth need not always result in complete comprehension; but it is perhaps worth noting.

And we must remember that, imposing as were the settings of Conrad's novels, they are, in essence, no more than the background influencing the thoughts and actions of his characters. Allowing for his devotion to artistic integrity, it was human beings who fascinated him – did he not give as the motto of *Youth* these words from Grimm's *Fairy Tales*, 'But the dwarf answered: No; something human is dearer to me than the wealth of all the world' – and almost every word he wrote about any of his characters had a bearing on its interpretation and development.

Therefore my book is designed to be psychological rather than literary, although, within its scope, I hope I have achieved some literary effect. Criticism is concerned with all kinds of aspects, and if purely literary criticism of creative writing is the first essential, other aspects have their uses. The many quotations with which, as I have said, I have been able to elucidate and enrich my text prove Conrad's rare insight and marvellous mastery of description, and my method of approach has enabled me to devote much more space to individual figures than would have been feasible in a literary appraisal of the novels as novels.

But nevertheless it could be argued that as a novel is an entity, its characters should be judged as part of that entity, and that to discuss them one by one is to miss the point and do injustice to a work of creative art. But though the harmony and spirit of a novel are the sum of everything within it, it must surely be evident that one cannot really take characters out of their main context, for a discussion of one hinges on a discussion of others, and the underlying theme, not merely the external plot, inevitably emerges. Also, behind the theme the setting itself cannot but infiltrate. To isolate the figures would be ridiculous, even if it were possible, as they all derive their vitality from the web of circumstance in which they have their being.

But in saying all this, I do not lose sight of the truth that a work such as mine misses the finer significance of these novels – their power, their beauty, their ordered pattern, the inner core of their atmosphere. Conrad himself wanted his novels to be judged as whole compositions – he disapproved of quotations taken out of their setting and disliked the idea of an anthology of his writings – but as he often said to me that no man could escape his fate and as he wrote to me that I was 'the best friend my work has ever had,' I am sure he would have looked with indulgence on this effort, as, indeed, he looked with indulgence on other efforts of mine in the same direction. In the years since his death there has been an immense body of criticism dealing with his books, to which, in the ordinary way, I do not feel I could add much of significance; but though there will always be fresh things to say about his work along those critical lines which include everything, my special branch of criticism will probably arouse less competition and, in the fullness of the analysis, backed by Conrad's own words, may perhaps be said to break new ground.

And more ground might have been broken, and perhaps to better effect, had I been able to do what, in some ways, I would have wished to do – select the most outstanding figures from all his novels and short stories. But it would have resulted in a much more inconsequent book than this. The present work is a reasoned essay on a definite plan, but to pick and choose, dodging here and there, while exciting for the writer, would have been bewildering for the reader. And yet what characters I have had to omit! However, the over thirty characters examined here, while naturally not all of them among my most favourite, yield a rich harvest, and I am sure I have done the right thing.

How did Conrad regard the six novels examined in this work? To some extent, but only to some extent, I can answer this question by what he wrote in his Author's Notes and in his letters, by what he jotted down in copies of the books belonging to myself and by conversations I had with him. I have no doubt that I could, by gradual and cautious enquiry, have ascertained many of his views more precisely; but, to begin with, it did not enter my head to do so and, secondly, Conrad was not the type of man to make such mental comparisons. In fact, his statements about his work did not always coincide, partly because his opinions probably varied and partly because he had to use sensible discretion. But I will do my best to present his ideas, mentioning these novels in the order of their publication.

Although in his Author's Note to *Lord Jim* (1900) Conrad did not commit himself to any particular view, remarking, 'As a matter of principle I will have no favourites; but I don't go so far as to feel grieved and annoyed by the preference some people give to my *Lord Jim*,' yet in a copy belonging to me he wrote, 'When I began this story, which some people think my best – personally I don't – I formed the resolve to cram as much character and episode into it as it could hold. This explains its great length, which the tale itself does not justify.' In that same Author's Note, he admits that it was begun as a short story 'concerned only with the pilgrim ship episode,' and then laid aside for a while; and if my memory serves, he informed me that this is what it ought to have remained.

Conrad considered *Nostromo* (1904) his principal creative achievement. The book took him some two years to write and I am sure he was bitterly disappointed at its tepid reception, due mainly, I fancy, to the fact that his public had come to expect of him the special atmosphere of the East and did not want him to write about South America. Praise of *Nostromo* was always pleasant to Conrad – it was actually by writing an article on it that I got to know him – and though I would not call it his favourite novel, which position was held by *The Nigger of the Narcissus*, not on literary but on personal grounds, yet he put it in a place apart. As he wrote in a copy of mine, 'My feelings on re-reading it can best be expressed by the French saying, *Ne fait pas ce tour qui veut.*'

For *The Secret Agent* (1907) Conrad had a considerable regard. In this novel he had succeeded in doing what he set out to do, which was, as he wrote in my copy, 'to treat consistently a melodramatic subject ironically.' Indeed, away back at the time of its publication he admitted the same thing in a letter to R. B. Cunninghame Graham: 'It had some importance for me as a new departure of *genre* and as a sustained effort in ironical treatment of a melodramatic subject – which was my technical intention.' No false note breaks the symmetry of this design, though I did once venture to point out to Conrad that such a man as Verloc would surely never have used such a word as 'hyperborean.'

I have a feeling, perhaps unjustified, that Conrad's liking for *Under Western Eyes* (1910) had something slightly defensive about it. One of his reasons for writing it was, as he wrote in my copy, to counteract 'the rubbishy character of stories about Russian revolutionists published in the magazines,' but he found the composition of the novel hard going and, as he wrote to

Norman Douglas at the time, 'there's neither inspiration nor hope in my work.' And yet, more optimistically, he wrote to John Galsworthy, 'it is not an easy work but it may be rather good when it's done.' I am not certain whether he ever thought it more than 'rather good.'

Of *Chance* (1913) Conrad apparently had a good opinion to begin with, but later on, not so good. In a letter to J. B. Pinker at the time of its completion he said, 'As to what *it is* I am very confident. As to what will happen to it when launched – I am much less confident.' But in after years he thought that people had overrated it. But there was a tendency in Conrad, a very natural tendency, to speak well of his less successful novels at the expense of those that had been widely praised, and it may be that if *Chance* had not been such an enormous triumph, he would have had a better notion of it. In my copy he wrote, 'In this book I made an attempt to grapple with characters generally foreign to the body of my work and tried to treat them colloquially,' and my impression is that, however he may have judged the book as a whole, he was not dissatisfied with the result.

Victory (1915) was assuredly one of his novels that Conrad liked particularly. He might, I believe, have written of it as he wrote of *The Mirror of the Sea* in my copy, 'I have a special feeling for these pages,' for he *did* have a special feeling for it. He took immense pains with this work, the writing of which occupied him more than a year and a half, and I remember him telling me that over the conversation between Ricardo and Schomberg, which fills nearly three chapters, he toiled for either a month or six weeks. Conrad was fond of discussing characters in *Victory* – how he laughed when I reminded him of Schomberg and Zangiacomo, glaring at one another, as they drove down to the port in a gharry looking for Heyst and Lena! – and it was easy to see that he had a real affection for this book.

On re-reading these six novels for the purpose of my study, I find that my own views of their respective quality have altered to some extent. *Lord Jim*, as a novel, does not stand as high as it did, although the earlier part, the part meant originally to be a short story, is as splendid as ever; *Victory*, so alive in its characterisation, so moving in its drama, stands higher than it did; *Under Western Eyes*, never one of my favourites, seems, though containing magnificent passages, to miss that something which makes all the difference. I am aware that some critics would place it first of all his novels, but I am afraid I cannot agree with them. As for *Nostromo*, I still hold it to be Conrad's greatest effort; as for *The Secret Agent*, I still rank it near the top; and as for *Chance*, the finer things in it appear finer then ever, but it seems to me that there are sections which rather drag. I could, of course, enlarge on these various points in an effort to justify my conclusions, but when all is said, what appeals to any particular reader may be beyond precise argument. And anyhow I am only speaking relatively.

To revert to what I was saying earlier, it is probable that not Conrad alone but most serious novelists build many of their characters from countless hints on which they embroider. But a majority of such hints are weak and indecisive and get lost or forgotten. It is only now and then, and often with the aid of the author himself, that precise facts are revealed and we obtain definite glimpses of real people. So let us see what, in this respect, we can gather about the origins of Conrad's figures.

The story of *Lord Jim*, in so far as Jim's desertion of the pilgrim ship is concerned, was obviously common property throughout the East when Conrad was there, and in his Author's Note to this book he writes: 'One sunny morning in the commonplace surroundings of an Eastern roadstead, I saw his [Jim's] form pass by – appealing – significant – under a cloud – perfectly silent. It was for me ...... to seek fit words for his meaning.' We are not told who he was, but as it was presumably at the time of the official Enquiry in Singapore that Conrad saw him, if the local papers for that period were ransacked everything would surely come to light. Whether any of the other figures in the novel were founded on ascertainable facts is uncertain – when I get to *Victory* I shall have something to say of Schomberg, who makes a very brief appearance here – but J. D. Gordan in his work, *Joseph Conrad, the Making of a Novelist*, says that the second half of *Lord Jim* owes much, both in outline and characterisation, to incidents in the life of James Brooke, the first white Rajah of Sarawak. Conrad, I know, was interested in the Brooke family, and I recall how pleased he was when I arranged a lunch party at which he would have met the Ranee Margaret of Sarawak: unfortunately the plan fell through owing to the indisposition of one or the other. I cannot say whether Stein was known to Conrad, but it is morally certain that his collecting butterflies and beetles was suggested by a reading of A. R. Wallace's *Malay Archipelago*, one of his favourite bedside books, as Conrad himself cared less than nothing about natural history. I have always suspected that Captain Brierly, who presided over the official enquiry, was based on a real man, for his tragic story, isolated from the main current of the novel, has a curiously authentic ring. Could he, too, I wonder, be traced? And perhaps that old rascal, Captain Robinson, had been seen by Conrad, as he also sounds uncommonly real. Who knows? As for 'Gentleman Brown,' I shall have more to write of him when I discuss 'Plain Mr. Jones' of *Victory*.

[19]

Of *Nostromo*, we learn from the Author's Note that Nostromo himself was founded on Dominic (a real person) of *The Mirror of the Sea* – as Conrad remarks, 'Many of Nostromo's speeches I have heard first in Dominic's voice' – and that his stealing of the silver ingots one by one was suggested by an episode in an old book of travel. And we also learn that Antonia Avellanos was an echo of his first love. (All the same, it is Mrs. Gould who is much more the image of his ideal woman who, in different novels, appears (as it seems to me) in the Protean shapes of Doña Rita, Winnie Verloc and Mrs. Travers.) But while these scraps of information are thrown to us by Conrad, it appears rather strange – or it would appear rather strange if I did not know, from long experience, the queer way in which his memory worked – that Conrad did not tell us that many of the surnames in this novel came straight out of a book by G. F. Masterman published in 1867 and called *Seven Eventful Years in Paraguay*. Masterman was a doctor at the General Hospital in Asuncion, the capital of the Republic, and was imprisoned under the dictatorship of the ruthless Lopez. In this work there are such names as Carlos Gould, Decoud, Captain Fidanza (Nostromo's real name), General Barrios, Michell (spelt without the 't'), and Monygham who, like his namesake in *Nostromo*, was put to torture – all of them outstanding figures in the novel. The Father Beron of *Nostromo* is represented by Father Roman, but both of them exist largely to hear the confessions of prisoners and both utter the repeated words, 'Will you confess?' There can be little doubt that Conrad read this book, recommended to him perhaps by R. B. Cunninghame Graham, who was in Paraguay shortly after the death of Lopez and many years later wrote a study of him, published in 1933, in which he mentions Masterman's work. If such was the case, Conrad must automatically

have memorised the names, for it is quite certain that he completely forgot the source and more than likely even forgot that
he had ever seen them in print. His memory was very erratic: it
could be piercingly acute about impressions, it could be utterly
vague, or actually non-existent, about facts. But of one thing
I am quite sure: he would *never* have used a group of names from
a book which, in some directions, covered much the same
ground as *Nostromo* had he had the slightest recollection of the
circumstances. (Of course, it is conceivable that, searching
round for South American names, he was given those by someone, probably Cunninghame Graham, but there are various
details connected with them which make this sound improbable.)

From the Author's Note to *The Secret Agent* we can gather
some facts, but little is known of the true origins of most of the
characters. That Sir Ethelred was drawn from the Home
Secretary, Sir William Harcourt, Conrad acknowledges – Sir
William's precise words, quoted in the Note, 'your idea of
secrecy over there seems to consist of keeping the Home
Secretary in the dark,' are repeated almost verbatim in the text.
In another paragraph he says that 'the suggestions for certain
personages in the tale, both law-abiding and lawless, came from
various sources which, perhaps, some reader may have recognised' – and maybe some reader did then, though time has
worked its customary havoc. But it is possible that he was
referring to one of those 'certain personages' when he wrote to
R. B. Cunninghame Graham, 'Mr. Vladimir was suggested to
me by that scoundrel Gen. Seliwertsow whom Padlewski shot
[in Paris] in the nineties.' With regard to the Greenwich explosion, a friend (apparently Ford Madox Hueffer) told Conrad,
'Oh! that fellow was half an idiot. His sister committed suicide

afterwards,' thus accounting for the presence of Winnie Verloc and her brother Stevie. As regards Stevie, Conrad must have taken his description from what *The Times* said of the youth who had been blown up: 'He could hardly have been more than twenty-two. His hair and moustache were silky and fair, he had no beard, his eyes were blue:' it is an almost speaking likeness. As for Winnie, while I have no facts to go on, my feeling is that Conrad had a definite model. For she was, as I have said before, one of his ideal women and he must surely have seen her somewhere: a touch of reality is essential to recreate an absorbing image of the past. He also tells us in his Note that he had read the 'rather summary recollections of an Assistant Commissioner of Police, an obviously able man . . . . . . who had been appointed to his post at the time for the dynamite outrages in London away back in the eighties' – so here, no doubt, is the germ of the Assistant Commissioner of the novel, though the Greenwich explosion did not take place till 1894.

The Author's Note to *Under Western Eyes* is almost blank on the subject of originals, although it is obvious that Mr. de P—, whom Haldin assassinated, was the Minister de Plehve – Conrad admits it in a letter – who was killed by a bomb thrown at him in St. Petersburg in 1904 by a revolutionary called Sazonov. At the time, presumably, Sazonov's personality and background were discussed in the press, and it would be interesting to know whether the portrait of Haldin was based upon them. It also seems likely that General T— was intended for General Trepov, a notorious Russian reactionary of that era. It has been suggested that Kropotkin gave hints for Peter Ivanovitch, and as Conrad might have met him through Edward Garnett, who was acquainted with this Russian anarchist, it may have some foundation. But, at the best, it is a slender theory. And I dare say that, during Conrad's stay at Champel near Geneva, he may have come in contact with some man who suggested the teacher of languages – G. Jean Aubry in his *Joseph Conrad: Life and Letters* states that the idea of the novel 'sprang out of a casual conversation he had had with a stranger in Geneva as long ago as 1895' – and that he possibly met various Russian émigrés who furnished hints for other characters. But all this is supposition.

With one exception, no one seems to have tracked down, with certainty, any of the originals of *Chance*, though I rather suppose that Fyne and possibly Anthony were suggested by real people. I can imagine some friend of Conrad's introducing him to a neat, reserved, stocky little man with the remark, 'Mr. — is a Civil Servant,' just as I can imagine that Anthony, idealised as he may be, recalled an actual sea captain of his acquaintance. This is only assumption, of course, but I often feel that when Conrad pays particular attention to detail, expending an extra wealth of creative care on one of his figures, some sort of memory lurked at the back of his head. One seems to learn his 'touch,' and though this may be illusory, it leaves an ineffaceable impression. But it would be carrying things too far to include every striking figure in such a generalisation, as that would soon degenerate into a mere guessing game. The one character of *Chance* for the reality of whom there is a positive clue is de Barral. He was, apparently, a composite picture of several financial swindlers who flourished in London at the end of the last, and at the beginning of the present, century. The flamboyant one I have in mind took, as de Barral took, the whole floor of an hotel for his offices; and the effacing one seems to have led as obscure and drab a personal life as did de Barral. Conrad was interested in the psychology of such men and discussed them with me at various times.

In his Author's Note to *Victory* Conrad informs us that Lena, Heyst, 'Plain Mr. Jones,' Ricardo and even Pedro all had their shadowy beginnings in people he had come across. It was in a café of a town in the south of France – somewhere else he explains that it was the Café Riche at Montpellier – that he saw Lena playing in a little orchestra, just as Heyst first saw her when she was playing in a little orchestra at Schomberg's hotel in Samarang, and afterwards, when she went round collecting money, heard her 'very charming' voice. Perhaps it was this voice, most of all, that enshrined her in his memory, for was it not its lovely tones that enchanted Heyst? Conrad does not tell us where he met Heyst, who was a Swede as in the novel, but he was affected by 'the mere amenity of his detachment,' which was 'too great to make any claims, big or small, on one's credulity.' But he does tell us that it was in an hotel in the West Indian island of St. Thomas that he met Mr. Jones: he was resting on three chairs 'all alone in the loud buzzing of flies to which his immobility and his cadaverous aspect gave a most gruesome significance. Our invasion must have displeased him because he got off the chairs brusquely and walked out, leaving upon me an indelibly weird impression of his thin shanks.' This recollection was a singularly vivid one, even to the detail that the Mr. Jones of St. Thomas was also a gambler, and I fancy that he may have had him in view, as perhaps 'Gentleman Brown' of *Lord Jim*, when, speaking of wanderers as a class, he said in an Introduction he generously wrote for a little book of mine called *Into the East*, 'I have known amongst them men of ruffianly mental complexion, cultivating a truculent manner and a cold steady stare, who, if it were possible to bluff one's destiny, might have been sitting in high places.' Ricardo, whom he met 'during a four days' passage between two places in the

Gulf of Mexico' and who regaled him with an 'exposition of his moral attitude toward life illustrated by striking particular instances of the most atrocious complexion,' would now and then 'give me a glance and make the hairs of his stiff little moustache stir quaintly. His eyes were green and every cat I see to this day reminds me of the exact contour of his face.' As for Pedro, who was encountered apparently somewhere in the same region, in some obscure way Conrad aroused his anger, and this 'bestial apparition . . . . . . fixed my conception of blind, furious, unreasoning rage, as manifested in the human animal to the end of my days.' All these silhouettes excitingly recall characters from *Victory*, but that is as far as we can get with them and their names are irretrievably lost. Schomberg makes no appearance in the Author's Note, but he is mentioned in the Note to the First Edition, where Conrad says of him, 'That I believe him to be true goes without saying. I am not likely to offer pinchbeck wares to my public consciously.' This amounts to a virtual admission of having known a man who was, to say the least, decidedly like Schomberg; and, indeed, nothing is more probable than that he had seen just such an hotel keeper in some Eastern port, possibly in several Eastern ports, as Schomberg keeps appearing in different places in different books.

None of the six novels, probably the most celebrated novels Conrad wrote, I have considered in this work is among his more autobiographical – for something approaching sheer autobiography in his novels one must consult *The Arrow of Gold* and *The Shadow Line* – and therefore the number of prototypes is seldom as satisfying as could be desired. And yet, such as they are, they do prove that, in some directions, the hold upon Conrad of his earlier years was strong and poignant. Few novelists have been endowed with a discernment so concen-

trated as to fan into fervent animation such distant remem-
brances; but then, few novelists have had the genius to be
attracted, in the grand manner, not alone to the interplay of
personalities and the problem of their ramifications, but to the
tide of life itself flowing from the past into the present in such a
resistless surge as to enlarge our horizons and deepen our sense
of the potentialities of fiction.

But this is not to say that all his characters are equally successful
and that I have not had, on occasion, to pick my subjects. Even in
Nostromo, where his creative power was so supreme, I do not
think that either Antonia Avellanos, courageous and noble as she
was, or Martin Decoud, whose writings paved the road to the
Occidental Republic, have that inner glow, that throbbing
individuality, which other of the principal actors in this novel
display so superbly. Why this should be so is hard to understand,
for it is obvious that Conrad spent infinite pains upon them, but
I can only suppose that, unless the fault be in myself, certain
types proved less amenable to his imaginative grasp than others.
It is not that those two characters are insignificant – far from it –
but that they lack, as I see them, that imponderable, precious
alembic which is so all-important. But this, I admit, is a personal
opinion – so personal, in fact, that in his Author's Note to
Nostromo Conrad reveals that of all the figures in this novel
Antonia is 'the only one who has kept in my memory the aspect
of continued life.'

But when Conrad's creative powers were at their zenith he
was, indeed, as J. M. Robertson said of Shakespeare, a 'great
magician.' Even now, despite the many years since first I read
his novels, I have been deeply moved when studying the
characters anew for the purpose of this book. They crowd upon
me, those children of one man's brain, I seem to know them

intimately; and though their creator, who was more impressive than any of them, has long been dead and there are, alas, fewer people every year to remember him, they are as fresh and timeless as when I first made their acquaintance. Conrad wrote that 'all passes and all changes,' but these figures neither change nor pass.

I

LORD JIM

1900

JIM

THE FIGURE OF LORD JIM – Tuan (Lord) Jim, as the Malays called him – after whom this novel is named, so dominates the scene from beginning to end that the subsidiary characters, clearly drawn though they are, seem almost dwarfed in comparison and have for the reader a certain tenuity even when directly linked with the life of the principal actor. The theme is so absorbing that the one man it concerns carries, in the intense vividness of his portrayal and the wide sweep of the canvas, the whole of its weight upon his own shoulders.

Brought up to enter the Mercantile Marine, Jim (no surname is given) was efficient at his work aboard the training ship and liked by his companions, who little suspected that this down-to-earth youngster had his own secret dreams. But actually his inner existence was largely compounded of such dreams: 'He saw himself saving people from sinking ships, cutting away masts in a hurricane, swimming through a surf with a line . . . . . . He confronted savages on tropical shores, quelled mutinies on the high seas, and in a small boat upon the ocean kept up the hearts of despairing men.'

To what extent he really believed in his capacity for courage in any circumstance and to what extent it was a sort of unconscious gesture of resolution to ward off a lurking fear of himself is beyond enquiry, but it is true that on the one occasion at this period when he might have justified his faith in himself he did fail. On a winter's night, in the clamour of a gale, the cry 'Man the cutter!' caught him unprepared, and for a moment 'he stood still as if confounded.' Thus, by that moment of indecision, he missed being in the rescue boat. But surely, in the light of what happened subsequently, it is a typical trait that when 'he saw the boat, manned, drop swiftly below the rail' he 'rushed after her.' Nobody supposed that his failure was due to anything but bad luck, and although he himself 'felt angry with the brutal tumult of earth and sky for taking him unawares and checking unfairly a generous readiness for narrow escapes,' he soon put it all behind him and remained convinced, as he fancied, that 'when all men flinched, then – he felt sure – he alone would know how to deal with the spurious menace of wind and seas.'

A few years later, 'gentlemanly, steady, tractable, with a thorough knowledge of his duties,' he became a very young first mate of a fine sailing ship, but unfortunately – or *was* it unfortunately? – was 'disabled by a falling spar at the beginning of a week of which his Scottish captain used to say afterwards "Man! it's a pairfect meeracle to me how she lived through it." ' Jim 'spent many days stretched on his back, dazed, battered, hopeless, and tormented as if at the bottom of an abyss of unrest.' Yet lying there in the utmost discomfort, he was 'secretly glad he had not to go on deck.' Sometimes, indeed, 'battened down in the midst of a small devestation,' he was filled 'with a despairing desire to escape at any cost.' But when the good weather returned 'he thought no more about it.' In the physical condition in which he was, his sensations during this week should not be accepted too literally, but undoubtedly Conrad introduced this unobtrusive episode, so easily missed by readers of Lord Jim, as a pointer.

Owing to his injury Jim had to leave his ship at an Eastern port, but after his release from hospital he took the temporary job of chief mate of the *Patna*, 'a local steamer as old as the hills, lean like a greyhound, and eaten up with rust worse than a condemned water-tank.' In this unseaworthy vessel, 'commanded by a sort of renegade New South Wales German,' he started to cross the Indian Ocean with eight hundred Mohammedan pilgrims, men and women, all bound for Mecca.

Up till the very instant of disaster the voyage had been one of perfect and unruffled calm, described by Conrad with superb eloquence, and Jim, in his musings, felt 'something like gratitude for this high peace of sea and sky. At such times his thoughts would be full of valorous deeds: he loved these dreams and the success of his imaginary achievements . . . . . . There was nothing he could not face.' Then, all at once, out of the secure serenity of the night, the accident happened which was to alter the whole course of his career. The ship struck what was probably a sunken wreck and 'the sharp hull driving on its way seemed to rise a few inches in succession through its whole length, as though it had become pliable, and settled down again rigidly to its work of cleaving the smooth surface of the sea. Its quivering stopped, and the faint noise of thunder ceased all at once, as though the ship had steamed across a narrow belt of vibrating water and of humming air.'

The white officers, staggering from the impact, knew immediately that something serious had happened, and Jim, who had kept his head, rushed to investigate: the vessel, now stopped, had evidently been badly holed as the forepeak was already half-full of water, and, more sinister yet, he felt the iron bulkhead bulge under his hand and, as he looked at it, a large flake of rust fell off. And now, with the swiftness of tropical weather-changes, an opaque cloud, presaging a storm, 'had eaten up already one-third of the sky' – and the seven lifeboats on board would not have held more than a third of the passengers! But unlike the other officers, a nondescript and dubious set of men, Jim did not give way to panic. True, he raised no alarm, for what would have been the use, but he set to work to 'cut the lifeboats clear of the ship,' while the other officers, in a frenzy of terror, were desperately trying to launch one of the boats in order to escape before the *Patna* sank, which might happen at any moment. Jim would not help them, for which he was cursed. But when, the boat being at last launched and the surviving officers safely in it – the acting third engineer, an elderly man, had died from a heart attack – the ship began to plunge in the rising sea and he heard, standing alone on the bridge, the captain utter a shout of warning, scarcely aware of what he was doing – at least, he said to Marlow, 'I had jumped ...... it seems' – he did jump overboard and scramble into the boat.

And at that very second he knew, with all its implications, just what he had done – betrayed his trust. He 'saw vaguely the ship he had deserted uprising above him, with the red side-light glowing large in the rain like a fire on the brow of a hill seen through a mist. "She seemed higher than a wall; she loomed like a cliff over the boat ... I wished I could die" he cried. "There was no going back. It was as if I had jumped into a well – into an everlasting dark hole ... " ' The fatal moment had again caught him unawares. On the previous occasion, the captain of the training ship had seized hold of him as he 'seemed on the point of leaping overboard;' on this occasion the restraining force was the physical impossibility of regaining the ship.

Her lights had now disappeared – the explanation, unguessed by them, being that 'when the squall struck her a little on the quarter, she swung head to wind as sharply as though she had been at anchor' – and all the men in the boat believed she had gone down, the chief engineer even adding that he had seen it happen. Without Jim's consent but without his active opposition, they agreed on a story to this effect, although the details they gave were sheer invention. Perhaps Jim would have held out had he not imagined, erroneously, as it happened, that he had heard shouts for help. And also, of course the lights *had* vanished: only one explanation could account for that! As he assured Marlow, 'The lights *did* go! We did not see them. They were not there. If they had been, I would have swum back – I would have gone back and shouted alongside – I would have begged them to take me on board . . . I would have had my chance.' Such words hardly agree with what he had said shortly before and rather suggest a semi-delirious effort to convince himself. And yet, crouching in the boat with the appalled realisation of what he had done, is it not just conceivable that he *might* have risked everything to regain his honour?

As we know, by some miracle of chance the *Patna* did not sink, but was discovered by a French gunboat and towed into Aden, when the whole truth, leading to an official Enquiry, emerged.

All this preliminary account fills approximately the first third of *Lord Jim*, the remaining two-thirds, summarised very briefly, consisting of Jim's efforts to rehabilitate himself. It was a difficult, tortuous road he had to carve out, all the more difficult and tortuous because of his temperament, though it was this very temperament of idealistic extremism which, if it made him abnormally touchy and scrupulous, also gave a heroic tinge to his single-mindedness.

What makes it so hard to follow Jim into the recesses of his mind is that he was not, in the accepted sense, much of a talker and can scarcely explain to Marlow, his only confidant, his train of reasoning and, even when arguing interminably with himself, lacks that clarity of judgment which might have simplified his problem. Admittedly, when Marlow gets to know him at the time of the Enquiry and, through his unsentimental humanity, gains his confidence, he does speak at length, trying with all his might to analyse his emotions and acts, but he is not always coherent. For example: 'It is all in being ready. I wasn't; not – not then. I don't want to excuse myself; but I would like to explain – I would like somebody to understand – somebody – one person at least!' The fact is, he genuinely wished to go fully and fairly through the whole incident, but he also wished, not exactly to exculpate himself, but to convince Marlow that it was not his real self which had made him behave as he did. And even as he was thus talking, another, a silent, voice was whispering something quite different and there was a gnawing at his heart. As Marlow, a very astute observer, remarks, 'He would be confident and depressed all in the same breath, as if some conviction of innate blamelessness had checked the truth writhing within him at every turn.' Is it surprising that presently he burst forth, 'Ah! What a chance missed! My God what a chance missed! . . . . . . But the ring in the last "missed" resembled a cry wrung by pain.'

He was only twenty-four, and though extremely sensitive, he was not, save emotionally, subtle; while he knew what he was seeking, he could not see matters in just proportion. Brooding alone for weeks before the Enquiry, as he had done, his mind had got tangled up – Marlow alludes to 'the mist of his feelings' – and his thoughts were whirling round in circles. Without Marlow's help he might have gone completely to pieces, for he had no prospects, he was practically penniless, and hope was only a fitful glimmer. But even though he was helped in every direction, his pride, all the more sensitive in the feeling that he had abrogated his right to possess any, caused his various employers much annoyance and disillusionment. For judged by the usual standards, his behaviour was frequently ungrateful and callous. Fleeing from any reminder of the *Patna*, he would leave job after job where he had made himself respected, where he had been a success, with no more explanation than a formal note or a few muttered words. So fervent was his longing to justify, somehow, somewhere, his own inner vision of himself that any breath of his tainted past acted as an inexorable goad, driving him to escape from the threatening shadow.

And yet all this was but a development of a characteristic which, in much milder manifestations, must always have been with him: like so many idealistic dreamers he was basically egocentric. Even his boyhood musings had, in their very nature, to do with his own glorification, however bound up with humanitarian motives. And even his resolution to drown out the past by some splendid feat had, apart from his bitter pangs of conscience, an underlying, if unknown, urge, which was to stand at last triumphant upon a pinnacle. And thus his determination to regain the right to look all men in the face could not but accentuate, in a sense, this inherent trait. For if the feelings and convenience of his employers meant so little to him when he felt pursued, even if he was also ashamed that he had not been frank with them, he had also apparently cut himself off from his doting old father in England without a word and, at the close of the book, tore himself away from the girl to whom he meant so much in order to fulfil his obligation to his dream. The greater did not include the less and, believing himself an outcast, he was unthinkingly ready to drag others into his pit of misery or, at the very least, grossly inconvenience and bewilder those who had befriended him. But in the everlasting perturbation of his mind, with its definite neurotic tendencies, one must not exaggerate a characteristic that, if selfish at times, was not without nobility.

He had a debt to pay, and this was the only thing that mattered when it came to the point. Very early, at the close of the enquiry, during which he had not attempted to embroider facts in his own favour, he said to Marlow, 'Something's paid off – not much. I wonder what's to come?' It was his recurring theme to the only man he trusted, and on different occasions he said to him, 'Some day one's bound to come upon some sort of chance to get it all back again;' later, 'I am bound to fight this thing down – I am fighting it *now*;' later still, after throwing up a particularly good post, 'I preferred to go . . . . . . This thing must be buried;' and even when he had been two years in Patusan, 'The very thought of the world outside is enough to give me a fright; because, don't you see . . . . . . because I have not forgotten why I came here. Not yet!'

But bad luck certainly did dog his footsteps, first in the form of the second mate of the *Patna*, then in the form of an overheard, derogatory conversation, and then on and on – 'more than I could count on the fingers of my two hands,' as Marlow re-marked, speaking of the jobs Jim had abandoned – and it is little wonder that he began to get a queer reputation and that his so zealously guarded secret became well known throughout the enormous reaches of the Orient.

Jim was unaware of this, for from the very first he was deter-mined that nobody should insult him to his face, as witness his fury with Marlow when, during a recess of the Enquiry and before they were acquainted, the elder man's observation, 'Look at that wretched cur,' was taken by him as a personal affront, whereas, in fact, it did merely refer to a mongrel that was running in and out of the crowd. And when, at length, he learnt from the mouth of a drunken Danish sailor in Bangkok that his secret was common property, it was soon clear to Marlow that his only hope was to get him right out of civilisation. His 'exquisite sensibilities,' as Marlow called them, made of life a menacing hell winding into the future, and it was then he had the idea, as a final resort, of introducing him to Stein, owner of many trading concessions, the idea that led to remote Patusan, to his boundless success, and to his death.

It has been suggested that, in creating Jim, Conrad instinctively endowed him with the introspection of an intellectual Pole, thus charging his character with infinite shades of meaning alien to the average Englishman who, however ashamed he might have been at his behaviour, would have got the better of his active remorse in time and been able to live out his life in relative peace of mind. But surely the problem Jim presents is a universal one, and surely degrees of mental fastidiousness can be found in every nationality and in every class. What Conrad was intent on doing was to probe to the very core the mingled good and bad, weakness and strength, which can struggle for mastery in any human soul. This is an elementary way of stating it, but it holds good because it covers everything. Being a great psychologist, Conrad understood the problem; being a great novelist, he clothed it in the semblance of humanity; being a great artist, he made it moving and impressive.

That Jim was an outstanding type is obvious, but because so much is told of his one ghastly failure, and largely by himself in his unceasing effort to recover the ultimate truth of his personality, we are apt to forget that even before his last act of sheer heroism he almost habitually exhibited high qualities of fortitude and fearlessness. We know that he retained his sense of duty on board the *Patna* up to the all-decisive moment; we know that he was prepared to knock Marlow down and did throw the Danish sailor who had insulted him into the river; we know that he used to go out in a small boat in the worst of weathers to get trade for Egström & Blake; we know that he overcame grave dangers to reach Doramin; we know that, later, he calmly risked being poisoned, and bearded four murderers, killing one and disarming the others; we know that with an 'untroubled bearing' he spoke to the horrible Brown, who admitted afterwards that Jim 'couldn't be scared,' across the creek in Patusan and appeared quite unconcerned when that nightmarish figure from the outer world announced that all the time one of his men was close at hand 'with a bead drawn on him.' Indeed, his career, judged impartially, was for the most part bold to foolhardiness. But in his own mind, until the close, everything was nullified by the one slimy blot upon his reputation.

The location of Patusan is left vague in the novel, but Conrad told me it was assumed to lie on the south line of north-west Sumatra. It was somewhere up-river that Jim finally settled, a strange, hazardous place in which, from being little better than a fugitive, he came to be the leader. He had fallen among a people who were both primitive and complex – primitive in the lack of civilised reactions and amenities, complex in the obscure undercurrents of feuds and jealousies. His existence, exalted almost beyond credibility, arose from his determined energy, his sense of fairness, and his invariable success. His self-reliance was fostered by the people's faith in him, and the urge to prevail over the past and to justify himself to himself seemed to surround him with an invulnerable halo. The untutored Bugis regarded him almost as a god, for never once had he failed them, never once had the mysterious white man ceased to exercise his beneficent powers on their behalf.

We must appreciate all this if we are to understand what the arrival of the cutthroat Brown and his gang of lawless scum meant to Jim. There was no Marlow with him then to watch and note; all we know comes from the fragmentary recollections of his servant Tamb' Itam, from the girl, Jewel, who loved him, and from Brown on his death-bed far away. Did he feel that he had so mastered his destiny that he could meet this new and ominous threat with his now customary luck, or did this invasion from his abandoned world rock him to his foundations? From what we can piece together he was confident at first, perhaps on the principle that the after-effects of a hot bath can warm even in the iciest weather, but it seems plain enough that even before Dain Waris, his dear friend and the only son of his titular master Doramin, was shot, he had begun to lose his grip, not on immediate realities and how to face them, but on his belief that he had mentally escaped for ever.

For there can be little doubt that the conversation he had with Brown had an insidious and undermining influence on him. It did not alter his resolution, but, as Marlow says, it had the force of 'a menace, a shock, a danger to his work.' For, as he continues, 'there ran through the rough talk a vein of subtle reference to their common blood, an assumption of common experience; a sickening suggestion of common guilt, of secret knowledge that was like a bond of their minds and of their hearts.' It must almost have sounded to Jim as if this vile man had unmasked him and that he was, by innuendo, being dragged down to his

[41]

infamous level and, at any instant, might feel the past leap out at him.

Was this why, against the strong universal wish of the people whose life was his life, he permitted Brown and his companions to escape down the river instead of destroying them, who had slain several of the villagers, while they were yet in his power? In a sense it was, not because Brown had intimidated him, for he had done nothing of the sort, but because what he had said had made him feel, with a poignant thrust, that they were all erring men together. In his speech to the people, when insisting on his views being accepted, he had announced that 'they were evil-doers, but their destiny had been evil, too;' and to Jewel, who wanted them killed, he said, 'Men act badly sometimes without being much worse than others.' The weight of his secret was reasserting itself.

And it may be, of course, that beyond the reason he gave to the Bugis, a reason which they could be brought to understand, there may have been other reasons, which are not mentioned. Could he justify, in his own mind, the wholesale slaughter of all these men and might it not bring retribution in its wake? He saw the problem with a white man's brain, but to the native brain the problem must have been infinitely simpler.

And it should be remembered that, so far as Marlow could gather the ends together, Jim 'did not mistrust Brown,' having no experience of 'his revengeful rage of a thwarted autocrat,' when all he had asked for was a clear run to the sea. But nevertheless he arranged for the necessary precautions, appointing Dain Waris to take charge and have armed men posted on either side of the river. How could he have foreseen that Jewel's stepfather, the degraded Malacca Portuguese Cornelius, who had a festering hatred against Jim for having superseded him as Stein's agent, would get in touch with Brown and, by piloting the boat-load of men through a side-channel, enable them to catch Dain Waris and his warriors in the rear, murder some of them, including Dain, and then get safe away down river to their ship ? Fate once more had turned against Jim.

His plan had finally won approval because hitherto everything he had promised had come to pass, as by a magic touch, and so when he stated, 'Everybody shall be safe,' the words were accepted as meaning precisely that. But when, on hearing the terrible news from Tamb' Itam, he ordered an immediate vigorous pursuit only to be told that it would be unsafe even for his servant to appear in public, 'then Jim understood. He had retreated from one world, for a small matter of an impulsive jump, and now the other, the work of his own hands, had fallen in ruins upon his head.' He did not, as we know, really think that his 'impulsive jump' was a 'small matter,' but the bitterness of his defeat – and all is only Marlow's conjecture – may momentarily have transformed his morbid introspection, come to vivid life because of Brown's words, into a sort of baffled, weary rage against his misfortune. He knew at once what he must do, for indeed 'everything was gone and he who had once been unfaithful to his trust had lost again all men's confidence,' he must go immediately to Doramin and face whatever was in store for him.

He was probably under no illusions. His prestige had vanished with a suddenness and completeness as sinister as it was stunning, for he understood these people, their simplicity and their violence, he understood all that his son meant to Doramin. But this time he would not be caught unawares: 'The dark powers should not rob him twice of his peace.' And so he went to his death, tearing himself from the stricken Jewel, with the last fatal split-second of indecision already conquered, to pay his debt and create reality out of his cherished vision.

It was calmly and quietly that he appeared before Doramin, standing erect in front of that man, savage and remorseless in his inherited instincts, who believed him to be guiltily responsible for his son's death. ' "He hath taken it upon his own head," a voice said aloud. He heard this and turned to the crowd. "Yes, upon my head." A few people recoiled. Jim waited awhile before Doramin, and then said gently, "I am come in sorrow." He waited again. "I am come ready and unarmed" he repeated.' And Doramin, from whose throat came 'gurgling, choking, inhuman sounds' and whose 'little eyes stared with an expression of mad pain, of rage, with a ferocious glitter,' raised his pistol and, as 'Jim stood stiffened and with bared head,' shot him at close range. As he fell, he 'sent right and left at all those faces a proud and unflinching glance.'

'And' adds Marlow, 'that's the end. He passes away under a cloud, inscrutable at heart, forgotten, unforgiven, and excessively romantic. Not in the wildest days of his boyish visions could he have seen the alluring shape of such an extraordinary success! For it may very well be that in the short moment of his last proud and unflinching glance, he had beheld the face of that opportunity which, like an Eastern bride, had come veiled to his side.'

Marlow uses the words 'inscrutable at heart,' and surely, despite the fact that Jim's soul is bared for us with an intensity of perception with which few souls have been bared, he *is* inscrutable. Had he never experienced adversity it is likely enough that he would have remained no more than a competent ship's officer, his fancies gradually fading as middle age overtook him, and it needed the spur of disaster to bring out the hidden man.

The loftiness of his dreams clashed with a secret infirmity of his mind until, through an event outside his calculations, a new force was engendered in him. He had latent possibilities which might have slumbered all his life had he not, because of his own weakness, crashed to earth. Ruin for him was as the light seen by a convert, and through disgrace and anguish he found the road to freedom.

JEWEL

As THE ONLY WOMAN in Jim's life and practically the only woman in *Lord Jim*, the girl who passes under the name of Jewel would naturally call for attention; but, in fact, she is of interest in herself and well worth discussing. Brought to Patusan by her half-white mother as an infant, she knew nothing of any other place, and after the death of her mother lived a most wretched life with her disgusting step-father. Marlow could not imagine 'what notions she had formed of the outside world, for all her knowledge of its inhabitants were a betrayed woman and a sinister pantaloon. Her lover also came to her from there, gifted with irresistible seductions; but what would become of her if he should return to these inconceivable regions that seemed always to claim back their own? Her mother had warned her of this before she died . . .'

In the early perilous days, before Jim and the girl got emotionally involved beyond the point of recovery, she had saved his life by warning him of a plot against it and had even implored him to leave the country for his own safety, but by the time Marlow arrived in Patusan to visit Jim they were deeply wrapped up in one another. Their love, free of conventional inhibitions, was absorbing and protective, but while for her it was her whole life, for Jim it could only be a part of his life: his obligations to the people around him, with which was interwoven the recovery of his ideal self, had its hourly claims, and though this does not imply that she was not as dear to him as he was to her, it gave a questioning note to her restlessness. Her mother's dying words kept ringing in her ears, and she lived in a perpetual muffled dread, like an ache which, dulled, is ready to burst out worse than ever, that sooner or later she would be left desolate.

It must be remembered that, not completely white herself, her existence had been passed among people who had no white blood at all and practically no contacts with white people; and that, despite all her loyal devotion, all her instinctive and, as it were, plastic response to what Jim, the white man, stood for, her attitude to things had a savage background which inevitably swayed her. To her the world outside was full of infinite evil, and though she believed in Jim's love, yet, beyond her capacity for expressing herself, she was terrified that one day he would be drawn back irresistibly by the dark and powerful influence of the unknown universe whence he had emerged.

And she had guessed, largely no doubt from the thousand little signs which create a woman's intuition, that there was some brooding secret in his heart, although, being totally unable to comprehend the nature of white society, its way of life, its general approach to problems, she simply could not get hold of it. She tried with all her might to induce Marlow to explain it to her, but her words echo with her agonised bewilderment: ' "There is something he can never forget . . . . . . What is it?" She put an extraordinary force of appeal into her supplicating tone. "He says he had been afraid. How can I believe this? Am I a mad woman to believe this? You all remember something! You all go back to it. What is it? You tell me! What is this thing? Is it alive? – is it dead? I hate it. It is cruel. Has it got a face and a voice – this calamity? Will he see it – will he hear it? In his sleep perhaps when he cannot see me – and then arise and go.

[47]

Ah! I shall never forgive him. My mother had forgiven – but I, never! Will it be a sign – a call?" '

In an effort to reassure her, Marlow was reduced to giving her an inkling of the truth, which anyhow she could never have grasped, in order to convince her, which anyhow would have been impossible, that Jim would never leave her, never be enticed back into the sphere he had left. Her sense of doom was impervious to praise or blame of Jim, both of which he tried, and he could no more have explained the real situation to her than a person blind from birth can be made to appreciate visual images. Indeed, the only result of his efforts was probably to deepen her suspicion that there were wicked, invincible forces beyond the seas, perhaps material, perhaps immaterial, against which she was beating her head in vain. It was not Marlow's logic, itself a part of his Europeanism and education, that was needed; it was some kind of direct demonstration which Jim, having the same Europeanism and education, could never vouchsafe her.

She must have felt at her wit's end before resolving to consult Marlow, for if Jim could not convince her, how could he? When Jim had told her he had been afraid, this being transparently un-true – there, quite apart from his proven courage, you have her accepted opinion that all men in so primitive and dangerous a land are brave–he must have said it to conceal the real truth! She even had the idea that Marlow's visit was mixed up with a desire to get Jim back, and in pitiful futility she asked him, 'Why did you come to us from out there? He speaks of you too often. You make me afraid. Do you – do you want him?' Marlow, seldom at a loss for words, was at a loss now. The more insistent he became, the more he floundered.

And yet these manifestations of her haunting fear, threading through all her musings, existed with such intensity only because her love was so intense. Marlow, observing her, said that 'her tenderness hovered over him like a flutter of wings. She lived so completely in his contemplation that she had acquired something of his outward aspect, something that recalled him in her movements, in the way she stretched her arm, turned her head, directed her glances. Her vigilant affection had an intensity that made it almost perceptible to the senses: it seemed actually to exist in the ambient matter of space, to envelop him like a peculiar fragrance, to dwell in the sunshine like a tremulous, subdued, and impassioned note.'

Such a description, at once beautiful and touching, might have been written of some English girl glowing in the light of her beloved; but Marlow, even before she spoke to him, as she finally did on the eve of his departure, noticed that Jim was 'jealously loved, but why she should be jealous, and of what, I could not tell. The land, the people, the forests were her accomplices, guarding him with vigilant accord, with an air of seclusion, of mystery, of invincible possession. There was no appeal, as it were; he was imprisoned within the very freedom of his power, and she, though ready to make a footstool of her head for his feet, guarded her conquest inflexibly – as though he were hard to keep.' Never for an instant, not even when in the softness of their love they sat, with arms entwined, looking into the night, did she feel safe, and though she fought to hold him, she could not lull her premonitions.

The thing about Jewel which leaves the most abiding impression, apart from her primitive inaccessibility, is the concentrated integrity of her character. In its mingling of ignorance and intuition, of passionate possessiveness and inappeasable fears, there is no trace of intentional exaggeration, and if she remains fundamentally obscure to our intelligence, her sincerity shines with absolute clarity. Brought up in a society with its own alien code of values, faced by a problem she could never assess, it was obvious that Jim would bewilder even as he fascinated, and that the more he tried to explain (as in the case of Marlow), the more would she be driven to suspect. But not for one second does she act a part: she is always herself, both in the tenderness of her affection and in the unforgivingness of her resentment. From our angle she may appear naive, but surely such a word is relative to a particular form of civilisation, and one could no more call her naive than, in her instinctive femininity, one could call her capricious.

In this girl, so devoid of guile and so full of life, so gentle and so fierce, the poison of the unknown was her greatest dread. She felt surrounded by deception which could not be countered. She had no woman rival to contend with, she had the impalpable seduction of the outer world to contend with. And with Jim this seduction was doubly potent: she was convinced, as I have said, that he was the slave of some *definite* secret which, when it called, would drag him away. She existed in a sort of nightmare in which, at any moment, the bell might sound, the fatal bell that would mean the end.

And that perhaps is why, when the bell did sound, her terror, wrought up beyond endurance, turned so imperatively and swiftly to frozen indignation. Speaking to Marlow at Stein's house, the thought of what was to her Jim's shameful desertion, when she would so willingly have died with him, sealing their bond in sacrifice, gave to her words the desperation of utter frankness. She no longer cared what she said, she no longer wanted an explanation. He had done this to her, and in casting her off he himself had been cast off. 'He could see my face,' she said, 'hear my voice, hear my grief! When I used to sit at his feet, with my cheek against his knee and his hand on my head, the curse of cruelty and madness was already within him, waiting for the day. The day came! . . . and before the sun had set he could not see me any more – he was made blind and deaf and without pity, as you all are. He shall have no tears from me. Never, never. Not one tear. I will not! He went away from me as if I had been worse than death. He fled as if driven by some accursed thing he had heard or seen in his sleep . . . ' It was the forlorn and furious cry of a devotion cheated and humiliated, the cry of a bitter mourning for ever uncomforted.

But for all her wrong assumptions, for all her inability to understand, she had hit upon the central truth. His dream came first! Never more for Jewel would there be anything but revolt, scorn and suppressed anguish. And that was Jim's reward, the only reward offered him by the world, for having paid his debt and been faithful to his vision!

'GENTLEMAN BROWN'

BROWN, who 'was supposed to be the son of a baronet' – he used to refer sneeringly to himself as 'Gentleman Brown' – is one of the most abominable figures in literature, and all the more abominable in that he had a diabolic capacity for ferreting out the weak points in others and could cunningly act a part which, while appearing not to make himself out to be other than what he was, gave a slant to his words and an air of frankness to his manner which could deceive even those who felt him to be an unspeakable scoundrel.

He and his gang of sixteen looters and murderers, with every man's hand against them, turned up in a starving condition off the coast of Patusan and, leaving a few men on board their stolen ship, started up the river in the longboat, a rabble of armed scarecrows, arriving in due course at the village where Jim had found his fame. 'Perhaps,' explains Marlow, 'he had heard of Patusan – or perhaps he only just happened to see the name written in small letters on the chart – probably that of a largish village up a river in a native state, perfectly defenceless, far from the beaten tracks of the sea and from the ends of submarine cables. He had done this kind of thing before – in the way of business; and this now was an absolute necessity, a question of life and death . . . . . . A cargo of produce for the schooner could perhaps be extorted – and, who knows? – some real ringing coined money! Some of these chiefs and village headmen can be made to part freely. He told me he would

[52]

have roasted their toes rather than be baulked. I believe him.'
We know all this, and a good deal more, because Marlow met
him later on his death-bed in a native Siamese hovel, and he
gloated over the news of Jim's death and the idea that he, himself, had been responsible for it. He told Marlow that he had
hated Jim at first glance. This, in itself, is not surprising, not
alone because of 'the other's youth and assurance, his clear eyes
and his untroubled bearing,' but because he saw at once that
'he had all the advantages on his side – possession, security,
power; he was on the side of an overwhelming force! He was
not hungry and desperate, and he did not seem in the least
afraid.' Before Jim, who had been up-country on Brown's
arrival, appeared, the freebooter, ensconced with his men on a
small knoll, had summed up the situation as eminently satis-
factory: 'The land already seemed to be his to tear to pieces,
squeeze, and throw away.' But the instant he met Jim he knew,
with his uncanny swiftness of perception where his own interests
were concerned, that the position was quite different from what
he had imagined and that guile must guide his steps until he was
ready to strike.

As I have remarked, for such a man in such circumstances hate
was natural enough, but there was also a pathological angle to it.
This brute, encompassed by a sort of phosphorescent trail of
evil, gloried in his deeds of darkness, and, having no edifying
view of his fellow men, could not believe that Jim, living in such
a remote hole, was not of the same kidney as himself. Why
would he be there unless to feather his nest, what was his shady
background, and how dare he, a complete fake, wrap himself up
in a mantle of moral superiority and treat 'Gentleman Brown' as
if he were so much dirt? This last thought roused seven devils
in him, and he would gladly have risked his own life if only, in

so doing, he could drag Jim down with him. But he must go warily, he must fool him!

And as we know, he did fool Jim to a limited extent – limited in one sense but, in view of the consequences, unlimited in another; and hearing of this from Marlow, 'his racked body writhed with malicious exultation at the bare thought of Jim. He exulted thus at the idea that he had "paid out the stuck-up beggar after all." ' He was dying – he died a few hours afterwards – but, in his ferocious loathing, the squared account, savoured luxuriously with death at his very elbow, meant more to him than anything else. Hear him in his raving hate: ' "I could see directly I set my eyes on him what sort of a fool he was," gasped the dying Brown. "He a man! Hell! He was a hollow sham. As if he couldn't have said straight out, 'Hands off my plunder!' blast him! That would have been like a man! Rot his superior soul." '

And yet, totally incapable as he was of understanding Jim's idealism, Brown had intuitively hit upon his weak spot, and while he would have despised his fine qualities, he knew how to stab him in the back by making out to Jim's face that they were nothing but a fraud. He saw what, within his range, it was possible for him to see, but one may assume that, even if Jim had looked different and had answered him in his own language, he would still have hated him, though perhaps not so venomously. Such a man as Brown was, in the unfolding of Jim's saga, a portent, and it might be argued, though rather fancifully, that though Jim let him go because of their common frail humanity, the real unconscious reason was because he perceived in him the agent of an inexorable nemesis.

Sheer wickedness, wickedness for its own sake, so to speak, is a difficult thing to appraise, but Brown came as near to being absolutely wicked as any figure in fiction. And yet he, too, had his weak spot: he was terrified at the thought of prison, although quite unafraid of dying. Maybe it had something to do with his hunger for wandering all over the East, spreading 'with a sort of senseless ferocity' disaster in his wake, or maybe he just could not stand the idea of being in the power of the law, which he had flouted all his life, and so be compelled to let his bloodthirsty longings boil in vain. As Marlow says, 'This man, who would stake his existence on a whim with a bitter and jeering reckless-ness, stood in mortal fear of imprisonment. He had an unreason-ing cold-sweat, nerve-shaking, blood-to-water-turning sort of horror at the bare possibility of being locked up – the sort of terror a superstitious man would feel at the thought of being embraced by a spectre.' Indeed, it was this fear which had made him flee from the Philippines in such a sorry state.

One cannot help a sense of satisfaction in learning of Brown's fear, which gives him some semblance to a human being, just as one cannot help feeling astonishment at hearing that he had once experienced the pangs of grief, which tends to increase that semblance. He had induced the wife of a missionary in Melanesia who, poor devil, 'had been heard to express the intention of winning "Captain Brown to a better way of life" ' – how loudly the hyaenas must have laughed! – to run off with him, when she was already desperately ill. And when presently she died, he 'shed tears over her body.' The mate of his ship, who was evidently not given to sentiment, observed that he had 'carried on like a big baby,' but as for the wretched woman, it was fortunate for her that she expired so promptly: that surprising mood would not have lasted.

This story of the missionary and his wife suggests, once again, Brown's capacity, already alluded to, for playing a part, not out of character apparently – this was the crafty touch – but with a kind of smothered hint of something better underlying his openly-confessed rascality. But had the missionary known the real Brown he would never, narrow, ignorant or fanatical as he may have been, have fostered the wild hope of bringing him to a 'better way of life;' and had Brown not known how to charm a woman of at least some education and background, he could never have aroused in her anything but appalled disgust. But Brown was not merely Bill Sikes, he was also Fagin: he had learnt how to play his cards, even if generally his cards were straightforward rapine and murder, and he had a force of personality that made him master, not alone of his rapacious crew, but of situations which required a certain delicacy of handling.

He lived only for himself, and though we are left in merciful ignorance of his youth – what we are told of his earlier manhood is atrocious – it is probable that he had always lived only for himself. He was born pitiless and he died pitiless – and invariably false. As Marlow sums him up, 'The corpse of his mad self-love uprose from rags and destitution as from the dark horrors of a tomb. It is impossible to say how much he lied to Jim then, how much he lied to me – and to himself always. Vanity plays lurid tricks with our memory, and the truth of every passion wants some pretence to make it live. Standing at the gate of the other world in the guise of a beggar, he had slapped this world's face, he had spat on it, he had thrown upon it an immensity of scorn and revolt.' Indeed, his hatred and contempt of mankind made him glory in being an outcast, even though an unsuccessful one, and in his stony heart thoughts of deception and violence were sweeter than thoughts of comfort and safety.

Well, at any rate he died true to his colours, even if those colours were steeped in filth and blood.

STEIN

STEIN was one of the three men – the others, of course, being Marlow and Brown – who were all-important in the moulding of Jim's last phase. He was, says Marlow, 'one of the most trustworthy men I have ever known,' and as he also had far-flung trading connections in some of the wildest parts of the East Indies, where an agent could utterly escape from the corroding memories of civilisation, it was, as we know, to him that Marlow went for advice and help when he decided that Jim's only hope lay in putting completely behind him any possibility of being reminded of the *Patna* and all she stood for.

The part Stein played in this drama was active in a sense, as it was through him that Jim reached Patusan and through him that he was given a house and supplies; but for the most part it was passive, and that is why, to our lively regret, we see so little of the man himself. For there is something particularly attractive about the gravely-humorous, intelligent, elderly Stein who, after a life of fabulous adventures, in which he had gained a fortune but lost a wife and child – as is not unusual with Conrad, he gives us a glimpse into his past, thus building up the picture of the man – was now living a patriarchal existence in his 'spacious house three miles out of town [Samarang in north-eastern Java] with an extensive garden, and surrounded by stables, offices and bamboo cottages for his servants and dependents, of which there were many.' He spent his spare time cataloguing his celebrated collections of oriental butterflies and beetles and corresponding with learned entomologists all over the world.

The wisdom of long experience tinged by a magnanimous outlook gave him subtle comprehension as a listener, and at the close of Marlow's narrative he summed up in a few words the quality in Jim which accounted for so much: 'I understand very well. He is romantic.' Marlow, as quick in his reactions as Stein, grasped at once what he meant, which was by no means the popular interpretation of that amorphous word. He meant, knowing the facts, that Jim was an injured perfectionist aiming high, a failure with his vision fixed on an elusive star, an imperfect human being who cared only to win a victory which would not only wipe out his past but justify some great ideal he had formed for himself.

Stein, expanding, continued in his Teutonic English: ' "If he tries to climb out into the air as inexperienced people endeavour to do, he drowns – *nicht war?* . . . No! I tell you! The way is to the destructive element submit yourself, and with the exertions of your hands and feet in the water make the deep, deep sea keep you up" . . . . . . He sat down and, with both elbows on the desk, rubbed his forehead. "And yet it is true – it is true. In the destructive element immerse" . . . He spoke in a subdued voice, without looking at me, one hand on each side of his face. "That was the way. To follow the dream, and again to follow the dream – and so – *ewig – usque ad finem* . . . " The whisper of his conviction seemed to open before me a vast and uncertain expanse, as of a crepuscular horizon on a plain at dawn – or was it, perchance, at the coming of the night?'

Put baldly – which, while it may clarify, loses, of necessity, those niceties of perception and phrasing which gave to the words their convincing impressiveness – it came to this: that Jim would have to start afresh in a new medium, struggle upward from nothing, while the essence of his dream matured into reality. That was Stein's idea, that was what led to Patusan – but would the result be dawn or night?

Perhaps the effect of the conversation on Marlow owed something to the room in which it was held. A curious ghostly feeling must have pervaded the huge study, glimmering in the dusk as with the sheen of countless insects in their glass cases, with Stein in the midst like the silent guardian of an incalculable treasure; and as night advanced that eerie feeling would increase in the semi-darkness. Marlow was vividly conscious of it, as Stein, rising to put away a rare butterfly he had been examining when he entered, passed 'out of the bright circle of the lamp into the ring of fainter light – into the shapeless dusk at last. It had an odd effect – as if those few steps had carried him out of this concrete and perplexed world. His tall form, as though robbed of its substance, hovered noiselessly over invisible things with stooping and indefinite movements; his voice, heard in that remoteness where he could be glimpsed mysteriously busy with immaterial cases, was no longer incisive, seemed to roll voluminous and grave – mellowed by distance.'

If my emphasis on the atmosphere of Stein's sanctum seems uncalled for in the general scheme of this work, the intention is to explain something both elusive and massive about Stein himself, the great adventurer to whom life was a still greater adventure, the dreamer surrounded by material objects which, in the processes of his thought, had become part of his dream, the realist who sought the road of truth through symbolic parables. This recluse, who was also a man of affairs, had an unusual personality and a wide understanding. Marlow says of his appearance that the 'gentle light of a simple unwearied, as it were, and intelligent good-nature illumined his long hairless face. It had deep downward folds, and was pale as of a man who had always led a sedentary life – which was indeed very far from being the case;' and the contrast it suggests is typical. Taken all together, his life and his conversation showed him to be the type of man, a type so seldom encountered, to appreciate the two sides of Jim, the realistic and the idealistic, without losing sight of the pitfalls of existence.

It was to Stein's house that Jewel, accompanied by the faithful Tamb' Itam, fled after Jim's death. Stein looked after her as a father, but her tone of unforgiving despair and of grief hidden in resentment deeply distressed him, for he could not make her understand Jim. 'Very frightful,' he murmured to Marlow, for in truth his philosophy had nothing to offer to that ravaged heart; and again, 'Terrible! Terrible! What can one do?' Marlow watched them walk together in the garden, but though there was charm in the picture, there was no hope: 'Her little hand rested on his forearm, and under the broad, flat rim of his Panama hat he bent over her, greyhaired, paternal, with compassionate and chivalrous deference. I stood aside, but they stopped, facing me. His gaze was bent on the ground at his feet; the girl, erect and slight on his arm, stared sombrely beyond my shoulder with black, clear, motionless eyes.'

It was natural for Stein to take an interest in this girl and natural for the girl to fly to his protection, for it was due to his influence that, years before, her mother had been able to find a refuge in Patusan from some disaster in her life alluded to by Marlow but left unexplained. But this interest covered Jim as well, and it must grievously have affected him, more especially as Jewel, like a perpetual reminder of sorrow, continued to reside in his house in a 'sort of soundless, inert' way, to know that his plan, developing with such brilliant achievement, had come to this. Perhaps, indeed, it accounts for the final lines in the book which tell us, in the words of Marlow, 'Stein has aged greatly of late. He feels it himself, and says often that he is "preparing to leave all this; preparing to leave . . ." while he waves his hand sadly at his butterflies.' It is a beautiful ending, so quiet in its perfection, so like farewell itself, but it rings sadly in the ears.

MARLOW

As all readers of Conrad know, Marlow appears as the narrator in a number of his novels and stories. To what extent he is to be regarded as an echo of Conrad himself, hovering over the scene and interpreting the moves, has been discussed by various critics (including myself, in times gone by) and from different angles. My own impression is that he is both a literary device whereby the narrative can be carried on and the motives analysed with added subtlety and fullness, and an extension of Conrad's own mind whereby his views of the characters and situations can be more justly appraised and presented. Through Marlow's watchful glance and unsleeping interest Conrad is able to get, as one might phrase it, under the skin of his figures, a trick which in Shakespearean days was achieved by asides and in Victorian days by an author's comments, thus building that atmosphere which is bound up with his own reminiscences and sense of values.

This is not to say that Marlow, as a man, is simply a dummy, for he has an individuality of his own, as indeed he has to have to be effective, and he plays his part with energy and enlightenment; but it *is* to say that, on the whole, there is a kind of shadowiness about him, a lack of essential detail, which, though he is often in the centre of events, keeps him outside the struggle. In fact, in the last resort he is there more as a historian, whose business it is to record convincingly, than as a participant, busy though he be. In short, for all his actuality, there is something of the disembodied sprite about him, a sprite with a cool, humane intelligence, who can pierce to the heart of things without getting really involved, however closely he may appear to be, in the unfolding drama. True, he has his likes and dislikes, he has his opinions and his prejudices, but so has every historian. Indeed, unless he had such emotions he would not be in the position to fulfil his role as tireless observer and possess that deeply-felt concern which causes people to confide in him. For in his presence all tongues are loosed, and Jim, Stein, Jewel, even the unspeakable Brown, bare their secret thoughts.

Marlow's existence permits Conrad always to be in the right place at the right moment or, at least, to find invariably someone to close the gaps, and if we consider that he is too ubiquitous or that nobody could remember, with such accuracy and eloquence, as much as he remembers, we are merely perceiving that there is no such thing as a perfect expedient. After all, it is only carrying one step farther the accepted mechanism of the novel as a work of art.

If Marlow is Conrad in disguise, it is clear that he is the mind of Conrad rather than the personality. And perhaps, even so far as the mind is concerned, he is, in a manner of speaking, only partially Conrad. For it is a mistake to assume that all his thoughts are inevitably those which Conrad would have had in like circumstances. The Conrad flavour pervades him, but as he has been granted his own personality, it follows that, within certain broad limits, he emits ideas or passes judgments as a man rather than as a puppet.

In so far as one is conscious of Marlow as a human being and not as a voice, one pictures him as mature and quiet, with a probing, ironic, generous mind and a friendly, uneffusive bearing. He avoids the obvious, he has acute sensibilities, he is absorbed by the problem of relationships and their results, but he does not obtrude himself and invariably behaves with that guarded frankness which makes him both approachable and reserved. And although he talks so much, mainly in retrospective monologue, it is as a listener that he really shines. As for his personal appearance, about which we are told next to nothing, it may be taken for granted that he looked just what he was, a ship's captain, entirely reliable and, at first sight, conventionally unremarkable.

All the characters of a novel are the children of their creator, but the connection between Conrad and Marlow, however one explains it, is obviously much closer than the usual one of author and subject. For if Marlow is a figure in his own right, he is also, as I have suggested, Conrad's roving eye. He turns up at the official enquiry in Singapore, at Stein's house in Java, at the settlement in Patusan, at Brown's deathbed in Bangkok, but then he *had* to turn up in these places, and various others, because Conrad *had* to be there. Acting as Conrad's agent, so to speak, he follows the trend of events and is never caught napping. But if he stands level with everybody in order to miss nothing, in some strange way he stands above everybody. His voice is heard throughout the book, but much of it is heard only by the reader, and so aloof is he from the hurly-burly, in which he may seem to be almost as omniscient as fate, that it is immediately apparent – yes, even to any person whose only acquaintance with him might be in *Lord Jim* – that the tragic network of events does not touch him personally as an actor, even if it may touch him personally as an observer. And surely this is so because he is present always for a purpose of his own – or, rather, Conrad's.

Throughout the preceding sections dealing with this novel, I have constantly quoted from Marlow, but this was to illumine the minds of others, even if, in so doing, it illumines his own, and yet it would be absurd to quote from him in this section. For all we know of Marlow is, I repeat, to be found in what he says about others, and while he discusses everyone, no one discusses him. At any rate, we do not hear such discussions as, in the nature of things, we cannot listen behind his back. Moreover, though the whole work revolves round him in one sense, in another sense he is not one of the characters and lies outside the perimeter. This, of course, must be understood in a special way, for Marlow, as seen by the other characters, would not strike them as different in kind.

Every creative novelist acquires a particular method, and Conrad, who was a master of technique and appreciated the value of the indirect approach, employed Marlow to say and do things which, from his point of view, would produce the best results. Whether Conrad originally intended to make Marlow his mouthpiece or whether, through the force of his status, Marlow could not help being his mouthpiece is a moot point, but in the outcome it appears to me that he is both things, if not, in every respect, completely.

It might be argued that more space should be allotted to a figure of such outstanding significance who, both in this novel and in *Chance* – a novel whose characters are analysed later in this book – is so constantly in evidence. But Marlow, in his special niche, does not present psychological problems and, I emphasise again, does not belong to the inner substance of these stories. (And that, incidentally, is why he occupies the last section here.) Indeed, there is little more call to discuss Marlow openly than to discuss Conrad himself. But as beneath the surface one *is* discussing Conrad all the time, so perhaps, to a lesser degree, is one discussing Marlow most of the time.

[65]

2

NOSTROMO

1904

NOSTROMO

THE ENORMOUS PRESTIGE OF NOSTROMO (Giovanni Batista Fidanza), founded upon his services to the community of Sulaco and his power over the populace, on his resource, reliability and courage, on his outstanding personality and fine presence, justifies the title of this novel, even if the book does perhaps contain more arresting figures. He was, indeed, a very remarkable man. Deserting from a Genoese sailing ship in order to better himself, this Italian sailor had not only risen to be the Capataz de Cargadores (Foreman of the Lightermen) of the port, but had developed into such a public character as to be universally known as Nostromo, which is simply an elision of the two Italian words *Nostro* and *Uomo* – 'Our Man.' (It was, we are told, Captain Mitchell's mispronunciation which resulted in 'Nostromo,' but it is perhaps worth noting that *nostromo* is the Italian for 'boatswain,' and that Fidanza had been the boatswain of the Genoese bark.) Captain Mitchell, under whose orders he worked, had appointed him to the post and had an immense opinion of him (not reciprocated by his subordinate) – and quite rightly so. As he declared, 'This Nostromo, sir, a man absolutely above reproach, became the terror of all the thieves in the town . . . . . That's what the force of character will do for you.'

Whenever there was need of a man of vigorous capacity and proven rectitude Nostromo was called upon, and his ostensible duties at the port were only part of his activities. When, for example, Sir John, the chairman of the railway company who were constructing the line between Sta. Marta, the capital in the interior, and Sulaco on the coast, came out from England to negotiate with the authorities and, in order to visit Sulaco before his return, had to travel over the rough mule tracks of the high Andes, it was Nostromo, in charge of a gang of men, who was selected to care for his security and comfort on that perilous journey in an 'old diligencia over impassable roads skirting awful precipices.' The great man had acknowledged his complete satisfaction in handsome terms. And when, not so many months later, the defeated Dictator-President Ribiera came fleeing across the mountains, it was Nostromo, at the head of his lightermen, who held off the mob and enabled him to escape to a vessel lying out in the gulf. It had been a touch-and-go affair, but it had succeeded, as everything Nostromo did succeeded. And therefore it was only natural that when it was resolved to move the silver treasure of the San Tomé mine, the refined output of six months stored on the harbour wharves, it was Nostromo who was chosen to sail the lighter, the idea being to steer her to a small port just outside Costaguanan territory, where a north-bound steamer would be instructed to pick the treasure up.

Nostromo accepted the commission, as he accepted every commission however difficult, but with a sense of smouldering anger. He had a craving to be 'well spoken of,' as he admitted to Martin Decoud, who was to accompany him – as the publicist of the temporarily lost cause and the herald of the new republic, he would have been shot out of hand as soon as the rebels reached Sulaco and must, for the time being, continue his propaganda from outside – but this craving, which he did everything to foster, was at odds with his resentment at being invariably involved in the most hazardous tasks. And the present task would be the most hazardous of all. To begin with, a troopship carrying Sotillo's rebels was known to be approaching from Esmeralda, and though it was expected that the lighter would be well out in the bay by then, it was really anybody's guess whether, in the darkness of the night, she could evade detection. But that was not the worst danger, the thought of which exasperated Nostromo.

He had to make contact at sea with the steamer which was to carry the treasure northwards, and as he said to Decoud, 'We must keep out in the open looking for her until we have eaten and drunk all that was put on board here. And if we miss her by some mischance, we must keep away from the land till we grow weak, and perhaps mad, and die, and drift dead, until one or another of the steamers of the Compania comes upon the boat with the two dead men who have saved the treasure.' It was no craven spirit that made him speak thus, it was a sort of ill-suppressed fury that, merely to make the rich richer, his life should be put to such jeopardy and his reputation for success should be tried too hard. And yet, of course, he would have been indignant had anybody else been chosen for this desperate venture.

But if the plan miscarried in detail, its main purpose, to save the silver, succeeded triumphantly, although no one but Decoud and Nostromo was to know this until near the end of the book and no one at all except Nostromo was ever to know where it was hidden. For misfortune early overtook them: in the intense blackness, with all lights out, the rebel steamer was heard, close by, feeling her way to Sulaco, now stopping, now starting up again, and all at once she 'struck the lighter obliquely, heeling her over till she was half-swamped, starting some of her timbers.'

Luckily they were not seen, such was the pall of darkness, but they had to make for the Great Isabel, the largest of the islands lying on the outer rim of the Placid Gulf, run the vessel ashore in a shallow cove, and bury the treasure near at hand. Decoud remained on the island; Nostromo, leaving the small dinghy behind and promising to return in a few nights, started to sail the leaking lighter back to the harbour. But presently it occurred to him that this was a foolhardy thing to do, as Sotillo, now in Sulaco, would probably have heard of the effort to get the silver away and would have him arrested at once, so he let more water in, sank the lighter, and swam for the shore.

What he learnt there amazed him. Unknown to either Decoud or himself a hide merchant, called Hirsch, who had been visiting Sulaco, was so overwhelmed by the terror of events that he had hidden in the lighter and his presence was only discovered when they were out in the gulf. They supposed that, at the impact of the collision, he had fallen overboard and been drowned, but actually he had been caught up in a piece of mechanism and hauled onto the steamer. Very soon, more dead than alive, he was telling Sotillo everything he knew or believed, which was that the vessel, carrying Decoud, Nostromo and the treasure, had been cut in two and sunk. But though Nostromo obviously could not guess this, Sotillo, with the idiotic craftiness of a man at once greedy and stupid, was convinced that the story of the silver having been removed was a mere ruse and that it was still somewhere within his grasp.

It was Dr. Monygham who gave him this information, and Nostromo did not disillusion him. At first he had evidently half-intended to tell him the real facts, as is clear from his spasmodic words, ' "The swimming was no great matter . . . . . . It is what went before – and what comes after that – ," but then he broke off, as though his thought had butted against a solid obstacle.' And when the doctor went on to observe that the whole enterprise had been a mistake, for if Sotillo had found the treasure he would probably have cleared off at once – tactlessly suggesting, though not meaning it literally, that it might have been a good thing if he, Nostromo, had surrendered the silver to the colonel – all idea of telling him what had happened vanished. Why should he confide in such a man?

Events were moving too fast for Nostromo to venture as yet near the Great Isabel. This did not worry him over-much, as there was a supply of food and, on the island, a stream of fresh water, but in any event all his energies were now centred on the greatest of his undertakings, his classic ride of four hundred miles to Barrios and his loyal troops away south in Cayta. It was the one hope left for the safety of Sulaco and its inhabitants and for the San Tomé mine itself which created the wealth of the province.

His mission accomplished, Nostromo returned to Sulaco with Barrios and his men. And it was then, when nearing the port, that he espied the lighter's dinghy floating empty in the gulf. To the astonishment of everybody he jumped into the sea, swam to the boat, and was soon once more on the Great Isabel. Decoud had vanished, the boat was blood-stained – he must be dead! And four of the silver ingots had also vanished. What was the answer to this mystery? He could not know, nobody could ever know, that driven out of his mind by long sleeplessness and silence – even the sea-birds avoided the Great Isabel – Decoud had put four of the heavy ingots into his pockets, gone on board the dinghy, shot himself, toppled over, and sunk beneath the waters of the gulf.

In some obscure way, Nostromo felt that Decoud, though

[73]

dead, had betrayed him – perhaps, more than anything else, because he had put him into such an impossible position. His reputation was based as much upon his incorruptibility as upon his prowess, and how could this ever be explained away? Indeed, might he not, through the sheer force of the evidence, be accused of foul play as well as of theft? But whether this occurred to him or not, swift upon his enigmatic discovery must have followed another thought that, for safety's sake, Hirsch's frenzied account of the lighter having sunk with the treasure must never be questioned. *He*, renowned as a swimmer, had saved himself, but Decoud had gone down with the silver. The silver! ' "I must grow rich very slowly" he meditated aloud.'

Men seek to find rational, and comforting, explanations for their actions, especially when such actions have a dishonourable flavour; but although the position in which he was placed was an appalling one and although, in a tight corner, the most level-headed of people can behave inanely, yet the reason Nostromo gave himself for keeping quiet was not the only reason, even if it is more than likely that had the tally of ingots been complete, the idea of theft would not have come to him. But the chance was thrown in his way and he fell, partly because he felt trapped, resentful and betrayed; partly because, born a man of the people, he had always detested the capitalism whose slave he held himself to be; partly because, though his overweening vanity would not be injured by the chance of war making him fail, he could not face the charge of having lost four of the ingots – as he said to Mrs. Gould when he lay dying, 'they would have said I had purloined them' – and partly because, at the back of everything, was the knowledge that now he could settle his personal account with society. And perhaps, too, so fateful a concatenation of events, all seeming to join in his behalf, may have touched, even in this free-thinking anti-clerical, a vein of peasant superstition and belief in omens.

Nostromo, as we know, had started on this venture in a disgruntled state of mind. Speaking to Dr. Monygham just before he left, he muttered, 'You people are all alike. All dangerous. All betrayers of the poor, who are your dogs;' and to Decoud aboard the lighter, 'Was it for a joke they woke me up from my sleep after two days of street fighting to make me stake my life on a bad card?' It is true that he spoke thus bitterly to these two because he was aware that their appreciation of his worth was not without reservations, which must have galled him, but it shows his attitude. And it was this attitude, drilling deeper and deeper into him every day, that was, with all its implications, at the root of his behaviour. He felt he was being 'used,' he felt it more and more, although his profound conceit of himself, his craving for public recognition, his yearning for the plaudits even of those he despised, made him undertake any task, however risky, he was begged to undertake. Like many people who keep their inner thoughts to themselves, unless forced from them in a crisis, his were apt to fester, and his wounded self-esteem coupled to his hatred of the prosperous made him confide in Giselle, his beloved, that the 'rich lived on wealth stolen from the people, but he had taken from the rich nothing – nothing that was not lost to them already by their folly and their betrayal. For he had been betrayed, he said, deceived, tempted . . . . . . He had kept the treasure for purposes of revenge.'

When this conversation took place, Nostromo, in his caution, had unremittingly carried out for several years his scheme of growing rich gradually and was now hopelessly in the toils of his undermining secret. Although it made him all the more

intent on justifying himself, which must have been the endless
burden of his musings, he sensed that, somehow or other, his
logic was vitiated by a flaw. He was uneducated but shrewd,
and if he did half-convince himself of the soundness of his
contention, he knew that, when all was said and done, he was
no better than a thief.

Decoud, who was very intelligent, in his cynical, man-of-the-
world manner, understood Nostromo up to a point, but argued
that he was 'made incorruptible by his enormous vanity, that
finest form of egoism which can take on the aspect of every
virtue.' But this generalisation, accurate within its radius, ignored the workings of an untutored mind in a situation beyond
its control: the very fear of *not* being thought incorruptible, for
instance, was enough, in all the circumstances, to make him
corrupt. Decoud regarded Nostromo's vanity as 'direct, uncomplicated, naive, and effectual,' but he did not perceive that
it held within it possibilities that were indirect, complex, subtle,
and, if apparently effectual, deeply disintegrating.

Nostromo's love of praise and the limelight ran counter to
his contempt of humanity, for though he was theoretically on
the side of the populace, it was not so much a personal feeling
as a gesture of dislike of the upper crust. His character was full
of contradictions, but it must always be remembered that he
really was what he was praised for being – a man of immense
resolution, tremendous courage, striking capacity and, in the
ordinary way, unimpeachable honesty. And it may well be said
that, once he found himself up to the neck in the hazards of some
exploit, the instinctive resilience of his nature made him enjoy
doing his best, even if, with one half of his mind, he wished he
had not been called upon. And certainly, though he was in a
very disgruntled mood when he undertook the task of contact-

ing Barrios, it was entirely through his exertions that, as we have heard, Sulaco was saved.

Years later, Captain Mitchell, describing the situation to a visiting guest, explained how, largely for the sake of the Goulds, the Chief Engineer of the railway had 'consented to let an engine make a dash down the line, one hundred and eighty miles, with Nostromo aboard. It was the only way to get him off. In the Construction Camp at the rail-head he obtained a horse, arms, some clothing, and started alone on that marvellous ride – four hundred miles in six days, through a disturbed country, ending by the feat of passing through the Monterist lines outside Cayta. The history of that ride, sir, would make a most exciting book. He carried all our lives in his pocket. Devotion, courage, fidelity, intelligence were not enough. Of course, he was perfectly fearless and incorruptible. But a man was wanted who would know how to succeed. He was that man, sir.' Yes, Nostromo *was* that man.

In the revived Sulaco, grown enormously in size and wealth and now the capital of the Occidental Republic, Nostromo was as famous a figure as ever, a national hero, but though his public life was as open as any man's could be – it *had* to be open in the effort to appease his inappeasable vanity – his private life, the slow removal of the ingots, the cautious disposal of them in distant ports, carried thither in the trading schooner he now owned, was secret as that of a mole, and even at the summit of his renown he brooded moodily over his position. Unfortunately for himself, Nostromo was 'subjective almost to insanity,' and as the bars of silver had weighed down Decoud for his plunge into the abyss, so, in their revenge, did they weigh down the man who had vainly tried to persuade himself that he had a perfect right to their possession. As Conrad puts it: 'He suffered through his fears as much as through his prudence. To do things by stealth humiliated him. And he suffered most from the concentration of his thought upon the treasure. A transgression, a crime, entering a man's existence, eats it up like a malignant growth, consumes it like a fever. Nostromo had lost his peace; the genuineness of all his qualities was destroyed . . . . . . His courage, his magnificence, his leisure, his work, everything was as before, only everything was a sham.' But he held high his head in public, and when Charles Gould, in recognition of his quite invaluable services, asked what he could do for him, his answer had an arrogant self-confidence: 'My name is known from one end of Sulaco to the other. What more can you do for me?'

And then one day, returning from the longest of his voyages, he found that the Great Isabel, the storehouse of his wealth, had been invaded: a lighthouse was being erected there. Certainly it was well away from the ravine where the dwindling, but vast, treasure was hidden, but how could he again make his solitary night journeys without the fear of being discovered? His mind, alert and swift as ever, hit upon the ideal solution: he would have old Giorgio Viola, the Garibaldino, appointed as keeper of the light. And through Captain Mitchell this was easily arranged, and Viola and his two daughters were soon installed on the island. Now he could safely visit the Great Isabel, for the Violas were known to be his oldest friends and it was generally understood that he would marry the elder daughter.

But the silver had not ceased to cast its evil spell upon him; the lordly Nostromo, a figure of glittering fame throughout Sulaco, the admired of the rich, the benefactor of the poor, had achieved his purpose by a double and dishonourable subterfuge: he had not wanted anyone on the island, and it was the younger daughter, the fair and flower-like Giselle, whom he loved, not the dark and passionate Linda. But though it was now safe to visit the ravine after stolen words with Giselle, words easy to obtain as Linda, the assistant keeper of the light, was often on duty, the clutch of the silver was still upon him: 'He had not regained his freedom. The spectre of the unlawful treasure arose, standing by her side like a figure of silver, pitiless and secret, with a finger to its pale lips.'

And even now, this silver, so secure materially, had yet to play its last card: mistaken by old Viola for Ramirez, the unacceptable suitor of Giselle, Nostromo was fatally shot. But anyhow his infatuation for the younger sister could not long have been hidden from the Garibaldino any more than it was hidden from Linda, to whom he was now affianced – another act of baseness to suit his convenience by justifying the increased frequency of his visits – and he was nearing the end of his tether. But as he had triumphed in his life, so did he triumph in his death: Linda's loud and despairing cry, 'I shall never forget thee. Never!' was 'another of Nostromo's triumphs, the greatest, the most enviable, the most sinister of all. In that true cry of undying passion that seemed to ring aloud from Punta Mala to Azuera and away to the bright line of the horizon, overhung by a white cloud shining like a mass of solid silver, the genius of the magnificent Capataz de Cargadores dominated the dark gulf containing his conquests of treasure and love.' A noble ending to a great and noble book.

It would be easy to argue that Nostromo's head had been turned by adulation, and that therein lay the whole cause of his downfall. But such an explanation would be perfunctory and omit more than it solved. His strength and weakness were alike an inalienable part of himself, to exalt or to devour, and if in one

respect he was a splendid man gone wrong, in another respect
the very goad of his vanity made him even more splendid. In
whatever role he had been cast he would have mounted to the
top, but being completely self-centred he would never have
been satisfied and would always have had a grievance against the
world.

CHARLES GOULD

S O M A T U R E, reserved and master of himself was Charles Gould
that it comes almost as a shock to learn that, at the time of the
Revolution in Costaguana, his age was only thirty. He was
naturally a self-contained man, probably a heritage from his
British ancestors, for though his grandfather had fought for
Bolivar and his father and his uncle had been born in Costaguana,
in manner and appearance he was extremely English, 'spare and
tall, with a flaming moustache, a neat chin, clear blue eyes, au-
burn hair, and a thin, fresh, red face,' looking, indeed, 'more
English than the last arrived batch of young railway engineers,
than anybody out of the hunting-field pictures in the numbers of
Punch reaching his wife's drawing-room two months or so after
date.'

But at heart he was a Costaguan, just as he was by nationality,
and his character and wealth made him the leading citizen of
Sulaco. His father had been ruined by the shameless demands of
successive Governments and his uncle shot under the savage
Guzman Bento, but with the help of an American capitalist,
who had been impressed by his 'implication of calm and implacable resolution,' the San Tomé mine had been developed and
was now the greatest single asset of the whole country. But he
was never a materialist in the accepted interpretation. To bring
order out of chaos, to build creatively so that the land he loved
would prosper, meant more to him than money; but if few

people understood him, he was universally respected even by those who were diametrically different.

But there was a particular idealistic streak in Charles Gould which was appreciated by no one but his wife. His resolve to succeed was, in a sense, a monument to his father, whose vain efforts to keep the mine going had worn him out. As he confided to her, 'Who knows whether . . . . . . the San Tomé mine may not become that little rift in the darkness which poor father despaired of ever seeing.'

Year by year he found himself more tied to the mine which, from every angle, was the core of his active life. He was sometimes lost in fits of absorbed abstraction which 'depicted the energetic concentration of a will haunted by a fixed idea,' and even when he said gently to his wife, 'the best part of my feelings are in your hands, my dear,' it was like coming momentarily to the surface of one reality from the soundless depths of another.

During his educational decade in Europe, his interest in mining, due, of course, to his background and to his correspondence with his father, had always been intense and he visited mines in different parts of the Continent: 'Abandoned workings had for him a strong fascination. Their desolation appealed to him like the sight of human misery, whose causes are varied and profound. They might have been worthless, but also they might have been misunderstood. His future wife was the first, and perhaps the only person to detect this secret mood which governed the profoundly sensible, almost voiceless attitude of this man towards the world of material things. And all at once her delight in him, lingering with half-open wings like those birds that cannot rise easily from a flat level, found a pinnacle from which to soar up into the skies.' It was the idealism of his passion, mysterious in the feel of the unspoken, that, opening her eyes, enchanted her.

Charles Gould, with his ingrained contempt for the corrupt politics of Costaguana, offending all his sense of the fitness of things, had managed successfully, by 'ransoming its way,' to do what his father had never managed to do – keep the mine free of politics. It was a great wealth producer for the whole Republic and hitherto, on these terms, it had been left alone. But now, with the scum of the country, all intent on feathering their own nests, approaching Sulaco from the mountains and the sea, he had resolved that neutrality was no longer possible and had gone over to the theory, propounded by Martin Decoud, of a new republic consisting of the Occidental Province.

Had he retained the accumulated silver horde lying in Sulaco, he might have been able, as Dr. Monygham suggested, to bribe himself out of trouble, but he was 'sick of bribing and intriguing merely to have his work left alone from day to day,' and, like his murdered uncle, had gone into the fight in 'defence of the commonest decencies of organised society.' This macabre and blood-thirsty Revolution outraged everything he stood for, and he was 'too severely practical and too idealistic to look upon its terrible humours with amusement, as Martin Decoud, the imaginative materialist, was able to do in the dry light of his scepticism.' Serious in his single-mindedness, resolute to deal with the incubus once for all, he was not to be deflected from the policy he had laid down.

Everything, life and property, was in deadly peril, but Charles Gould's collected manner remained exactly as before. Rather than see his mine grabbed by the riff-raff and all his schemes brought to nothing, he had arranged for it to be, in the last extremity, totally destroyed and 'was prepared, if need be, to blow up the whole San Tomé mountain sky high out of the territory of the Republic.' Meanwhile, however, he did what he could with his usual silent efficiency. It was his character, above all, that kept the outer fabric of society together, and when Antonia Avellanos, in the depths of her misery, said to him, 'It is your character that is the inexhaustible treasure which may save us all yet; your character, Carlos, not your wealth,' she was voicing, in moving words, what everybody felt. For this young man, through his own qualities, enhanced by the prestige of his position, had gained a moral ascendancy over the better sections of the community which no one thought of questioning.

But even that would have been of no avail at the last had not Barrios from the sea and Hernandez from the Campo arrived, with their troops, in the nick of time. The grotesque charlatan Pedro Montero (Pedrito), now in possession of the town, summoned him to his presence, and though he tried flattery to begin with, Gould was of the opinion that had he not, for his wife's sake, explained that the 'existence of the mine was bound up with my personal safety,' he might not have been allowed to return home. He told this to Dr. Monygham, in reply to a remark of his, and perhaps it was the tension of the moment that made this taciturn man add a few words about 'These Liberals, as they call themselves. Liberals! The words one knows so well have a nightmarish meaning in this country. Liberty, democracy, patriotism, government – all of them have a flavour of folly and murder.'

It was typical of Charles Gould that he would not even address Pedrito, the victor, as 'Excellency,' and this, together with his cold, precise manner, so different from the florid words of the other – how he hated 'empty loquacity!' – rather intimidated

Pedrito, and he even, feeling embarrassed, suggested that, after
the fashion of the Second Empire, titles might be created and
Gould be made 'Conde de Sulaco – eh? – or Marquis,' only to be
met by stony indifference. But as the days went by and he found
the mine-owner to be quite intractable, his offended dignity,
baffled greed, and knowledge that Gould had been friendly with
the Ribiera régime, brought out all his tigerish traits and finally
he had the future 'Conde de Sulaco' led out to be shot, a calamity
only avoided by the collapse of the Revolution at the eleventh
hour.

Charles Gould's determination to destroy the mine rather
than hand it over not only expressed, as Conrad says, 'the tenacity of his character,' and 'something of his father's imaginative
weakness' – but might it not be called, rather, a resolve to avenge
his father, if not in one way, then in another? – 'and something,
too, of the spirit of a buccaneer throwing a lighted match into
the magazine rather than surrender his ship,' but also (which is
more enigmatic) 'the remorse of that subtle conjugal infidelity
through which his wife was no longer the sole mistress of his
thoughts.' While it is impossible to assess all the reactions and
motives of any human being, I myself am persuaded that, though
deep in his subconscious some sort of half-formed remorse may
have weighed with him, he was consciously completely unaware of any such unfaithfulness. In his own way, he was a
dreamer, but his dreams were of a special kind, and where he
was dense, as dense as the most ordinary extrovert, was in taking
his wife too much for granted.

Even in men of great emotional fidelity this is one of the
commonest of mistakes, but though Gould did make this mistake it was hidden from him partly by the selflessness of his wife
and partly by the intensity of his vision in the tremendous

[85]

range of his activities. His qualities were there for all to see, his mastery, his uprightness, his high sense of duty, his rare abilities; but it was the defect of these very qualities, perceived by no one but Emilia Gould, Dr. Monygham and perhaps Decoud, which brought a sense of slow desolation to his wife's faithful heart. But Charles Gould was, as I say, totally unaware of this, and having no capacity for that type of introspection which examines the niceties of one's own conduct in the light of the feelings of others, would probably never have seen it. It was one of those domestic tragedies, all on one side, to which there is no solution.

Unless one has read *Nostromo*, Charles Gould, from a brief study such as this, might appear to have a rather wooden personality, not only incapable of acting a part, but, despite his success, with a positive ignorance of what was so essential – South American psychology. But this would be an error: he understood his countrymen perfectly, but, being always true to himself, saw no reason, if he ever thought it out, why he should pretend to sink to the level of the lowest, any more than he saw any reason why he should not dress as he chose, even if other men dressed differently – again, if he ever gave it a thought. Indeed, to read the book is to watch him emerge as one of the most vitally alive of all Conrad's figures. He dominates the scene by reason of the reality of his character. Beneath his calm exterior, beneath his balanced behaviour and his practical turn of mind, there lay a passion for his ideals which expressed itself solely in action. And everybody sensed that he was a man of power who used this power for good. It was the rough Barrios who said that had he been shot 'Sulaco would not have been worth fighting for,' and if the ostensible reason for these words was his knowledge that, in such a case, the San Tomé mine would have been blown up, he was well aware that Charles Gould was, in himself, the mainstay of the town. Everybody of any worth trusted him: the Caballeros of the Campo, the workmen of the mine, the citizens of Sulaco, Sir John himself, who said, 'He helped me to organise the surveying parties. His practical ownership of the San Tomé silver mine gives him a special position. He seems to have the ear of every provincial authority apparently ...... If you follow his advice the difficulties will fall away, because he wants the railway.'

When the Revolution was over and the San Tomé mine resumed the measured beat of its expansion, Charles Gould, of necessity, became more and more immersed in this enormous undertaking. Always a man of few words, he probably grew more silent than ever, with the silence of a man absolutely sure of himself, entirely lacking in pettiness or showmanship. The Chief Engineer of the railway once remarked to Dr. Monygham, 'Upon my word, doctor, things seem to be worth nothing by what they are in themselves. I begin to believe that the only solid thing about them is the spiritual value which everyone discovers in his own form of activity.' And perhaps the mine *had* come to assume for Charles Gould a 'spiritual value' which, all-unguessed by himself, had impinged irresistibly upon the finer essence of his married existence.

It is strange and sad that what had so much attracted the future Mrs. Gould in the first days of their acquaintance, his romantic love of derelict mines, as we have heard, and his calm, assured bearing – 'He had struck her imagination from the first by his unsentimentalism, by that very quietude of mind which she had erected in her thought for a sign of perfect competency in the business of living' – should, through the twist that time puts upon things, now have filled her with a deepening dismay. But

[87]

probably she understood very well why he was what he was, the inevitable development of what once he had been, and if the whole atmosphere of the Casa Gould was also growing quieter, despite the social entertainments which were part of Mrs. Gould's duties as the wife of the Administrator, it was with the stillness and dignity of a defeat that to most observers looked like a triumph.

In the early days when, as Conrad remarks, 'theirs was a successful match' – and to the world at large it always so remained – he had once said to her, 'a man must work to some end.' Even then the words seem to presage something she feared, for she frowned, not because of the words themselves, which were innocuous, but because of the vague, abstracted look on his face, as if already his mind were far away. And yet, such was her protective love, which gave more than it asked, that seeing him in 'his riding breeches, leather leggings (an article of apparel never before seen in Costaguana), a Norfolk coat of grey flannel, and those great flaming moustaches,' she immediately put her dread behind her to think, 'How thin the poor boy is! . . . . . . He overworks himself.' But perhaps, as the years passed, these words may have recurred to her again, to be answered in her heart, yes, but to what end? – wealth, fame, power – or happiness?

Although we see Charles Gould so clearly and are immediately impressed by the force of his character, it is very difficult to analyse him constructively, so free is he from ordinary weaknesses, so armoured at every point. To say that he is the slave of an idea is merely, in the usual implication, to mean that he is thorough through and through, and even to say that he made his wife unhappy is not so much to accuse him of imperfection, for in his own way he was completely loyal, but of that lack of imaginative insight which was the result (apart from his temperament) of too much concentration on 'material interests' – interests which for him, however, transcended the material and were therefore all the more insidious in their cumulative effect.

EMILIA GOULD

IN HER OWN WAY, a very quiet way, Mrs. Gould is the most enchanting of all Conrad's women characters. The influence of her humane, perceptive individuality seems to permeate the book, and when Dr. Monygham, her secret worshipper, says to himself, 'She thinks of that girl [Antonia Avellanos, whose betrothed, Martin Decoud, is supposed to have been lost with the silver] . . . . . . she thinks of the Viola children; she thinks of me; of the wounded; of the miners; she always thinks of every-body who is poor and miserable!' he is perfectly correct.

Coming as a young bride straight from Europe, Mrs. Gould soon accommodated herself to her new surroundings, and being at once sensitive and gracious, took her rightful place as the wife of Charles Gould without any conscious effort: 'Doña Emilia's intelligence being feminine led her to achieve the con-quest of Sulaco simply by lighting the way to her unselfishness and sympathy. She could converse charmingly, but she was not talkative. The wisdom of the heart, having no concern with the erection or demolition of theories any more than with the defence of prejudices, has no random words at its command. The words it pronounces have the value of integrity, tolerance, and compassion. A woman's true tenderness, like the true virility of a man, is expressed in action of a conquering kind.'

Before her marriage Mrs. Gould had led a singularly quiet life. 'An orphan from early childhood and without fortune, brought up in an atmosphere of intellectual interests,' it was when staying with a widowed aunt in Italy that she had met her future husband. He, too, as we know, was little given to speech, but soon she had enwrapped herself about his heart and when he received the news of the death of his father in distant Costaguana, he went immediately to her and his words, after a brief announcement of the fact, 'I've come to you – I've come straight to you,' must have sounded, issuing from this silent man, as a declaration of love welling up through his grief. Indeed, even at the beginning of their wedded life, before the spectre of the mine threw its shadow upon her, their deep devotion to one another must always have had a sort of voiceless quality, as if their feelings, hovering about them in the air, called for few demonstrative words. But such an understanding quietude, so beautifully complete when it is harmonious, can melt imperceptibly into the stillness of a vacuum, and as the years went by and her husband grew more and more absorbed in his work, she became insensibly aware that he was slipping away from her, imponderably slipping away, into some sort of rarified atmosphere where she could not follow him. The surface was unimpaired, the smooth flow of life encompassed their personal relationship without a ripple, but her happiness was being undermined as by a destructive blight.

Had they not been a childless couple, not only would her loneliness have found an anodyne, but Charles Gould himself would inevitably have been less withdrawn. Perhaps the glow of complete felicity would never have been recovered, for that is something which must be mutual in the hidden recesses of two minds, but it would have given purpose to her existence that, flowering outwards for others, was withering within her, and it would have fulfilled a need which was now doubly wanting. The emptiness of everything must have seemed to this woman, so full of capacity to give freely from the boundless riches of her heart, almost like a curse from heaven. Sitting alone at the apex of her career, admired and trusted, we have a tragic glimpse of her inner thoughts: 'She had hoped for a long, long time that perhaps – But no! There were to be no more. An immense desolation, the dread of her continued life, descended upon the first lady of Sulaco. With a prophetic vision she saw herself surviving alone the degradation of her young ideal of life, of love, of work – all alone in the Treasure House of the World. The profound, blind, suffering expression of a painful dream settled on her face with its closed eyes.'

(All Conrad's most attractive women are childless, and though this may be bound up with the situations to be developed, my impression is that it was designed for the purpose of centring all his study of their characters on their unfettered personalities.)

In considering such a person as Mrs. Gould, one must be careful not to idealise away her essential femininity or put her upon a pedestal aloof from human weaknesses. The void which hemmed her in was a deeply feminine reaction, difficult for a man to appreciate, in the intensity of a secret grief without a cure, in the feeling that every material advantage, even to the unsullied record of her husband, was all meaningless in the lack of something which could never be put into words but was of more significance than anything else. Many women, of course, feel a grievance against life; but if Mrs. Gould, in her unselfishness, was conscious of a grievance, it would not have been expressed by so crude a word, because what affected her was a corroding pain through which she would never have sought to justify her emotions.

Indeed, only once, when the heart-broken Giselle crouched,

weeping, beside her as Nostromo lay dying, did she, 'nervous and excited' – nervous because she had been summoned suddenly to this dreadful scene, excited by what he had hinted of the lost treasure – have 'the first and only moment of bitterness in her life.' She said to the distraught girl, ' "Console yourself, child. Very soon he would have forgotten you for his treasure." "Señora, he loved me. He loved me," Giselle whispered, despairingly. "He loved me as no one had ever been loved before." "I have been loved, too," said Mrs. Gould in a severe tone.'

It has been argued that this strikes a false note and that Mrs. Gould would never have spoken thus, but surely that is to misunderstand altogether the nature of womanhood in its stresses. She, also, had been defeated by the treasure, a slow defeat over the years, stealing joy out of her life; she, also, had known the stranglehold of the material. And thus, faced again by the whole tragic cycle, she came unexpectedly, exhausted as she must have been, to the end of her emotional tether and of that reticence she had guarded so closely. For she was not a bloodless saint who, in solving her own problems, could shed the light of an impersonal pity on all who sorrow; she was a suffering woman who, beneficent in her acts and intentions, carried perpetually within her an inconsolable grief.

Mrs. Gould, being naturally understanding and free of all affectations, readily adapted herself to the customs of her adopted country: 'She kept her old Spanish house (one of the finest specimens in Sulaco) open for the dispensation of the small graces of existence. She dispensed them with simplicity and charm because she was guided by an alert perception of values. She was highly gifted in the art of human intercourse which consists in delicate shades of self-forgetfulness and in the suggestion of universal comprehension.' And she had, in herself, a gallant approach to existence which, even in her unhappiness, kept her spirit outwardly undismayed, whatever trembling fears she may have had for her husband. On the eve of the revolution, when darkness is closing down, her bearing to Charles Gould, intent upon his dangerous gamble in removing the silver out of reach of the revolutionaries, is superb in its contained courage. But the cursed mine, which had done such irreparable harm already and might bring utter disaster on them all, made her say to him in a kind of backwash of her thought, 'Ah, if we had left it alone, Charley,' to which his answer, 'It was impossible to leave it alone,' brought her response – how much it must have cost her to say it! – 'Perhaps it was impossible.' She spoke slowly and as she spoke 'her lips quivered a little, but she smiled with an air of dainty bravado.' And a moment later she left the room 'with a brave assumption of fearlessness.' And yet her efforts had failed. It was the mine that was her enemy, impersonal and implacable, and it was the mine that was dragging them to disaster. Yes, her efforts had failed, for as the astute Decoud wrote to his sister, her 'mission is to save him from the effects of that cold and overmastering passion, which she dreads more than if it were an infatuation for another woman.'

Mrs. Gould's idea of a perfect marriage was of a partnership in which self would be swallowed up in giving, of an understanding to create and renew the glow of life, and it is witness to her extraordinary unselfishness that her own disillusionment never impinged upon her compassion for others. She did not behave thus as an escape – it was not an escape – but because it was in her nature to put others before herself. And yet, buried within her, unsuspected and repressed, her misery, like an incurable complaint, gnawed incessantly at her heart. In his incomparable words, Conrad describes her desolation in the midst of glory: 'With a measured swish of her long train, flashing with jewels and the shimmer of silk, her delicate head bowed as if under the weight of a mass of fair hair, in which the silver threads were lost, the "first lady of Sulaco," as Captain Mitchell used to describe her, moved along the lighted corridor, wealthy beyond great dreams of wealth, considered, loved, respected, honoured, and as solitary as any human being had ever been, perhaps, on this earth.'

There, at the height of her success, secure in her exalted position, she is as lost as if the Revolution had succeeded and her husband had been shot. And it was at this instant, as, after bidding farewell to the last of her guests, she was left to herself, that Dr. Monygham arrived to summon her to the Great Isabel at the urgent request of the dying Nostromo. It was thus that 'cloaked and monastically hooded over her evening costume, this woman, full of endurance and compassion, stood by the side of the bed on which the splendid Capitaz de Cargadores lay stretched out motionless on his back.' He wished to tell her where the buried treasure was hidden, but she would not allow him to speak of it. Had it not caused enough anguish already? Let it lie there undiscovered for ever, 'shining, incorruptible,' and hateful in the disaster it had evoked.

It may be that the barrier which had risen between Charles Gould and his wife was, viewing their personalities and the circumstances, inevitable, and that what had drained away the flavour of her life could not have been avoided. The feeling of emptiness and defeated hope was perhaps the very reverse of the medal whose face she had cherished, and it is possible that the relationship she had once shared was bound to perish. Nobody can answer such riddles, and least of all the actors concerned. That which draws people together, that which binds them for life, may have its underground, sundering power; and high ideals, in one direction or another, can bring about disaster as surely as shallow frivolity. Emilia Gould could no more have sought for explanations than Charles Gould could have understood their import, for both characters, in their instinctive rectitude and dignity, were far beyond any kind of pettiness. Thus was denied to them the last outlet of hope.

It is clear that Conrad had an enormous admiration for Mrs. Gould and intensely wanted to present her to us in her feminine, and therefore human, perfection. And in my opinion he marvellously succeeded. The stress he lays upon her loneliness, whose whole existence was radiant for others, awakens sorrow for her sorrow who should have known only happiness, and I would like to end this little study of her personality with what are, I am inclined to think, Conrad's most moving words about her – 'Mrs. Gould leaned back in the shade of the big trees planted in a circle. She leaned back with her eyes closed and her white hands lying idle on the arms of her seat. The half-light under the thick masses of leaves brought out the youthful prettiness of her face; made the clear, light fabrics and white lace of her dress appear luminous. Small and dainty, as if radiating a light of her own in the deep shade of the interlaced boughs, she resembled a good fairy, weary with a long career of well-doing, touched by the withering suspicion of the uselessness of her labours, the powerlessness of her magic.'

DR. MONYGHAM

DR. MONYGHAM, who was 'bitterly taciturn when at his best' and whose 'short, hopeless laugh expressed somehow an immense mistrust of mankind,' had probably never been an easy man to get on with. We know little of his earlier life, except that he had once been a surgeon in a regiment of the British army, but the fact that he appears to have thrown up this appointment to become, while still young, chief medical officer of the Costaguan army under the Dictator Guzman Bento suggests, though it does not prove, that a certain angularity of temperament may have motivated the change.

But it is quite possible, of course, that it was love of adventure and the promise of high position that induced him to accept the post, and it is also possible that at that time he was more conventionally sociable than later on. But this last is improbable, for he was not one of those men who could conceal his real feelings or opinions under a misleading manner, but invariably cultivated a sarcastic attitude which made people dislike him. And yet he was, in truth, extremely sensitive, too sensitive to be hail-fellow-well-met, and he also possessed a great fund of loyalty about which nobody knew anything.

And that is why the atrocious treatment he had experienced at the hands of the Dictator – who, from thinking well of him, suddenly, in his maniacal suspicion of everlasting plots, had him seized, tortured again and again, and left to 'decay slowly in the darkness of his grave-like prison' – had impressed a searing,

complex pattern on his brain. His whole being was poisoned
by the knowledge that, at the last, he had been unable to stand
up to the torture: even after years he could not banish from his
thoughts the face or the voice of the priest who had tortured him.

By suggesting, with immense reserve of power, what he had
endured and how it had affected him, Conrad lifts a corner of the
veil and, in so doing, gives us a glimpse of hell, lighting, as with
a baleful glare, hideous recesses of cruelty and evil. As he says:
'The doctor had been a very stubborn prisoner, and, as a natural
consequence of that "bad disposition" (as Father Beron called
it), his subjugation had been very crushing and very complete.
That is why the limp in his walk, the twist of his shoulders, the
scars on his cheek were so pronounced. His confessions, when
they came at last, were very complete, too. Sometimes on the
nights when he walked the floor, he wondered, grinding his
teeth with shame and rage, at the fertility of his imagination
when stimulated by a sort of pain which makes truth, honour,
self-respect, and life itself of little moment. And he could not
forget Father Beron with his monotonous phrase "Will you
confess now?" reaching him in an awful iteration and lucidity
of meaning through the delirious incoherence of unbearable
pain. He could not forget. But that was not the worst. Had he
met Father Beron in the street after all these years Dr. Monygham was sure he would have quailed before him. The contin-
gency was not to be feared now. Father Beron was dead; but the
sickening certitude prevented Dr. Monygham from looking
anybody in the face.'

It was loathing for himself, a contempt mingled with ghastly
recollections of intolerable suffering, that made him creep into a
shell of misery and shame. Nobody knew the facts, but when,
released at the Dictator's death, he retired, penniless and solitary,

to Sulaco, his surly manner and bearing of an outcast caused him to be avoided. And, indeed, Dr. Monygham did believe himself to be an outcast: he had 'made himself an ideal conception of his disgrace . . . . . . It was an ideal view, in so much that it was the imaginative exaggeration of a correct feeling. It was also, in its force, influence, and persistency, the view of an eminently loyal nature.' His feeling of horror at having confessed and the recollection of how his confession had been wrung from him had bitten into his mind, and as he limped about the town in a 'check shirt and native sandals with a water-melon under his arm,' his grim and forbidding expression cloaked the torments of a lost soul. Naturally secretive and silent, he was the last person to confide in any one, even had he supposed that confidences would be the slightest help, and thus this man, who had always been difficult, was shunned by all and left alone with his terrible thoughts.

But when Gould brought his bride back with him to Sulaco, everything changed basically. Dr. Monygham had known his father, and soon, perhaps under the persuasion of Mrs. Gould, he was appointed doctor of the San Tomé mine. Materially his position had vastly improved, but he was still regarded with aversion: 'He was recognised, but not unreservedly accepted. So much defiant eccentricity and such an outspoken scorn of mankind seemed to point to mere recklessness of judgment, the bravado of guilt. Besides, since he had become again of some account, vague whispers had been heard that years ago, when fallen into disgrace and thrown into prison by Guzman Bento at the time of the so-called Great Conspiracy, he had betrayed some of his best friends amongst the conspirators.' And therefore, despite the fact that 'nobody pretended to believe that whisper' and despite his friendship with the Goulds, he 'remained somehow outside the pale.'

Outwardly he continued to show the same indifference to people at large as he had always shown, but since he had got to know Mrs. Gould something had altered in him. Through her tact and instinctive understanding, through her unselfishness and compassion, she had aroused in this soured and embittered man a sense of devotion that knew no bounds. The hidden loyalty of Dr. Monygham, to which, in his anguish, he had once been untrue, had flowered with an ardour so intense that at the beginning of the revolution, when the lives and fortunes of the Goulds were in direst peril, he made a decision, known only to Mrs. Gould and to Nostromo, to pretend to have turned traitor and abandoned the Goulds in order that time might be gained for Barrios and his troops to arrive from Cayta. And this called for a highly risky imposture on the blood-thirsty Sotillo.

But he was ready for anything, and the recollection of what had happened to him before, his knowledge that the deception could not be maintained indefinitely, were brushed aside. What he had to do, and what he did do, was to make the greedily ferocious Sotillo believe that the silver ingots had been sunk in the harbour and could, of course, be raised by dredging – a desperate game if ever there was one. The plan was to tie down Sotillo to the waterside well apart from Pedrito in the town in the vague hope that Barrios would not be too long delayed, for had these two murderous rascals joined forces 'there would have been massacres and proscription that would have left no man or woman of position alive.'

He carried out his scheme to the letter, playing upon the avarice of the colonel, who wanted the silver for himself but dared not long stave off a meeting with Pedrito even by fulsome letters, dangling the treasure before his eyes, egging him on, although he knew that death would be his reward were Barrios held up. It was for Mrs. Gould he did it, and did it with a sort of exaltation. And it was only by a hair's breadth that he escaped death, for as the first of Barrios's transports entered the harbour, he was about to be hanged at 'the end of the after-derrick' of the vessel, from the decks of which men, for days past, had been optimistically dredging for the silver. Surely by this act of cold and lonely courage he atoned for anything he may have said when his body was being mangled by the bestial Father Beron.

Dr. Monygham's devotion to Mrs. Gould was selfless but jealous. He did not believe that anybody, including her husband, was good enough for her; and though, in a sense, he was loyal to the mine, that loyalty 'presented itself to his fifty years' old eyes in the shape of a little woman in a soft dress with a long train, with a head attractively overweighted by a great mass of fair hair and the delicate preciousness of her inner worth, partaking of a gem and a flower, revealed in every attitude of her person.' He was indignant with Charles Gould for mixing himself up in politics, thus bringing jeopardy to his wife, and moreover, 'at the bottom of his heart he felt an angry uneasiness before the prosperity of the San Tomé mine, because its growth was robbing her of all peace of mind.' As he said to himself, when enumerating those she befriended, 'No one seems to be thinking of her.'

Even when, towards the end of the book, he obtains a splendid position as Inspector-General of State Hospitals, Official Adviser on Sanitation to the Municipality and Chief Medical Officer to the Consolidated San Tomé Mines, the mellowness of success did not make him a more agreeable companion, because, as Conrad says so finely, 'What he lacked was the polished callousness of men of the world, the callousness from which springs an easy tolerance for oneself and others; the tolerance wide as poles asunder from true sympathy and human compassion. This want of callousness accounted for his sardonic turn of mind and biting speeches.'

But if inwardly more serene than for years past, with the image of Father Beron no longer troubling his dreams, his heart ached because the woman to whom he had given his undying devotion had seen her happiness slip away from her through her husband's absorption in his vast, expanding mine. On the day the Goulds returned to Sulaco from England, where they had been for long months, sitting with her in the garden of the Casa Gould, 'he devoured her stealthily with his eyes, which, luckily, were round and hard like clouded marbles, and incapable of disclosing his sentiments. His pitying emotion at the marks of time upon the face of that woman, the air of frailty and weary fatigue that had settled upon the eyes and temples of the "Never-tired Señora" (as Don Pépé years ago used to call her with admiration), touched him almost to tears.'

Such was his lot. He had survived fearful tribulations, he was prosperous, he was widely honoured, but the very adoration which gave meaning to his existence held in it the seeds of anger and unrest. For all his crabbed exterior and prickly temperament, Dr. Monygham had a tender, loyal and sensitive nature, and he mourned in rebellious silence over the deepening frustration and solitude of that woman for whom he had been ready to lay down his life. He was, at once, the most unselfish and the most mis-understood of men.

CAPTAIN MITCHELL

IN HIS MIXTURE of simplicity, self-importance and courage there are few more delightful characters in Conrad than Captain Joseph Mitchell, the superintendent of the Oceanic Steam Navigation Company at Sulaco. Known to the official and business world as 'Our excellent Señor Mitchell' and to the captains of the line as 'Fussy Joe,' Captain Mitchell was a 'thick, elderly man, wearing high, pointed collars and short side-whiskers, partial to white waistcoats, and really very communicative under his air of pompous reserve.'

He has several claims to our attention: it was he who discovered the merits of Nostromo and made him foreman of the lightermen – Capataz de Cargadores; he showed great and fearless energy in helping the Dictator-President Ribiera to escape and in getting the silver out into the bay; he played a minor, but plucky, part in the Revolution when seized by Sotillo; and finally, he was a well-known figure in Sulaco and, though recognised as a bore, was so kind (if peppery) and, for all his solemnity, so fundamentally unaffected and essentially balanced that he was generally popular: 'Liked by the natives for his good nature and the formality of his manner . . . . . . known for years as a "friend of our country," he felt himself a personality of mark in the town.' And he *was*, though the esteem in which he was held was tinged, at least so far as the Europeans were concerned, with a touch of amusement. But as his complacency was devoid of conceit and as he had a complete integrity of character, his standing in the community was a triumph of personality rather than a tribute to his intellectual equipment or his influence on the life of the city.

Conrad has drawn him with unfaltering skill as a human being, and before the book is finished he has become an old and valued acquaintance. And the very fact that he is so densely commonplace, a man as devoid of angularity as he is of originality, makes it all the more astonishing that he is so real. In some hands he might have developed into a caricature or a type, but he has been individualised as vividly as if he had been a man of outstanding gifts. And though the reader is fascinated by his rolling sentences, it is largely because he can, as it were, hear the very tones of his voice.

If Mrs. Gould, through the sheer humanity of her nature, lightens the tension of *Nostromo* in one way, Captain Mitchell lightens it in another by his naive loquacity and sturdy conventionalism. His lack of imagination soothes his little vanities, for it would never have occurred to him that he could be the subject of laughter, and his courtly attitude even to the unfortunate – as, for instance, when 'to the very last he had been careful to address the ex-Dictator as "Your Excellency," ' although, battered and distraught, he was fleeing for his life – makes one feel particularly sympathetic to this man, always true to himself even in a desperate crisis. Thus he disarms us as we smile, and his lack of humour and the wearisome stories he tells about the historic events in which he believed himself to have been so deeply involved make him all the nearer to us.

To outrage his dignity was the worst offence anybody could commit, and as he was also a faithful employee and friend and a brave man he faced the miserable Sotillo, who had had him ill-treated and had threatened him with death, with a contempt superb in its infuriated recklessness. When Sotillo enquires how he liked having been tied up, Captain Mitchell's retort, 'It is the most incredible, abominable use of power!' makes one want to cheer, just as his contemptuous 'Bosh!' to Sotillo's subsequent announcement that 'the very breath in your body belongs to me' makes one want to do the same, even while trembling for his life.

But if the Captain was carried away by his feelings, there was a foundation of good sense and general soundness in his nature – as, indeed, is obvious, or otherwise he could never have attained the position he held. As Conrad says, 'For all his pomposity in social intercourse, Captain Mitchell could meet the realities of life in a resolute and ready spirit. Now he had got over the first shock of the abominable treatment he was cool and collected enough. The immense contempt he felt for Sotillo steadied him.' He informed the greedy and illiterate colonel of the Esmeralda regiment, whose frantic desire was to lay hands on the silver treasure, 'No doubt it is well concealed by this time' – a very daring observation made with a special loyal purpose.

But he was bewildered by the colonel's knowledge, as he was apt to be bewildered by so many things that went on under his nose: 'Unfortunately, Captain Mitchell had not much penetration of any kind; characteristic, illuminating trifles of expression, action, or movement, escaped him completely. He was too pompously and innocently aware of his own existence to observe that of others.' In itself, this might be regarded as an annoying trait, but it was so much part of him and counts so little in the final estimation that it is, in fact, rather appealing. And despite all the danger he had been in and all the lack of fear he had shown, it is probable that he never referred to this later, save incidentally. For, as I have said, if self-important and vain of externals, he was basically modest and would doubtless have argued, without hesitation, that he had only acted as any one in his position would have acted. Maybe his lack of perception fortified his bearing, but in any case 'Captain Mitchell was not the man to enlarge upon mere dangers much.' What he longed to enlarge upon was the significance of the epoch in the moulding of which he saw himself as a definite figure.

But if we want – and who would not want? – to watch him in his glory we must read that chapter towards the end of the novel in which, the Revolution long since over and great prosperity come to Sulaco, capital of the new Occidental Republic carved out of Costaguana, Captain Mitchell, still the superintendent of a vastly enlarged establishment, is leading a leisurely life highly gratifying to his sense of dignity and his feeling for the rightness of things. He had weathered the storm, he had not been found wanting, and was fittingly rewarded: 'Regarded by the O.S.N. Company as an old and faithful servant, Captain Mitchell was allowed to attain the term of his usefulness in ease and dignity at the head of the enormously extended service. The augmentation of the establishment, with its crowds of clerks, an office in town, the old office in the harbour, the division into departments – passenger, cargo, lighterage, and so on – secured a greater leisure for his last years in the regenerated Sulaco.'

The picture we get of Captain Mitchell in those days is rather like the happy ending of a fairy-tale, and it warms our hearts. 'Attending easily to current affairs, welcomed in houses, greeted by ladies on the Alameda, with his entry into all the clubs and a footing in the Casa Gould, he led his privileged old bachelor, man-about-town existence with great comfort and solemnity.' But it was on mail days, when it fell to his lot to entertain some distinguished visitor passing through Sulaco, that he really blossomed forth in full glory. He would take his guest everywhere, descanting, as he went, on personalities and affairs in his most expansive manner, as, 'proud of his experience, penetrated by the sense of historical importance of men, events, and buildings, he talked pompously in jerky periods, with slight sweeps of his short, thick arm, letting nothing "escape the attention" of his privileged captive.' No wonder that by the time the day was over and the visitor about to return to his steamer, he was liable to be in a bewildered state and 'shivering with the pleasant anticipations of his berth.'

(Incidentally, this chapter, so joyous and so easy to read, was Conrad's creative device for picking up a hundred loose ends, not by a bare capitulation of facts but by rounding out the history of the land and its people between the Revolution and the rebirth of Sulaco, as, at the same time, he rounds out the story of Captain Mitchell.)

From one angle, Captain Mitchell is, of course, a figure of fun and intended so to be considered, always allowing for his reality; but from another angle, he is a vital character in *Nostromo* and one who could not be spared. Is it surprising therefore that when, retired from Sulaco to become, apparently, the engineer-in-chief of the O.S.N. in England, he called on the Goulds during their visit to London, Mrs. Gould felt she 'could have a cry' when he 'rambled feebly about "historical events?"' Even a less sensitive person than Mrs. Gould might well have felt the same.

3

THE SECRET AGENT

1907

VERLOC

As it is Verloc, the secret agent, who provides the title for this novel, it is fitting to consider him first, infinitely worthless though he was. But if, in a sense, the story hinges on him, it is only Conrad's ironic treatment of Verloc that makes him comprehensible as a figure to be taken seriously. This may sound contradictory, but nevertheless the method employed, while revealing the author's contempt, does present him as a human being. To have shown open scorn would have deadened our interest, just as to have written of him as a man who, however faulty, was struggling against fate, would have given us an entirely false conception of his personality.

Verloc was an utterly lazy, amoral hanger-on, with a vague international background – how well his very name suggests this last – who found his inevitable niche in a world of shady dealings and borderline activities. He was born thus and, as Conrad explains, 'had embraced indolence from an impulse as profound, as inexplicable, and as imperious as the impulse which directs a man's preference for one particular woman in a given thousand.' Not basically a real criminal, not basically anything at all except a good-for-nothing with sufficient brains to earn a livelihood without working for it, he had no roots whatsoever and was quite prepared to drift into any kind of doubtful undertaking, provided his own peace and safety were no more endangered than was tacit in the sort of society to which he naturally gravitated. And that is why, when he did get himself involved in a situation so hopeless that there was no loophole, he collapsed completely.

Even if Verloc had not happened to be the secret agent of a foreign power while pretending to be the friend and confidant of anarchists, he would still have been clandestine, a parasite on the fringe of decent society, where money can be acquired in various equivocal ways, and it is quite in keeping with his character that the shop he owned, largely as a blind, dealt mainly in goods of a rather dubious type. His mind was as shadowy as his existence, and, being without principles, he went through life in a hazy secretiveness, caring for nothing but his own comfort, of which his wife was a part, practically unaware of the other people in his own house and so egotistically self-centred that he never gave a moment's thought to their problems or personalities.

Conrad's delineation of Verloc's appearance is so vivid that, as we read it, we seem to be looking at the very man: 'His eyes were naturally heavy; he had an air of having wallowed, fully dressed, all day on an unmade bed.' And how clearly, having read this account, we can visualise him as, aloof from everything but his inward musings, he is shown to us sitting in the back parlour of his little house in that mean, dark, silent street, 'his hat pushed off his forehead, the skirts of his heavy overcoat hanging in a triangle on each side of the chair.' And perhaps, even if we had never heard his name, we too, meeting him on the pavement, might have been struck by that something all wrong which the author describes: 'He might have been anything from a picture-frame maker to a locksmith; an employer of labour in a small way. But there was also about him an indescribable air which no mechanic would have acquired in the practise of his handicraft however dishonestly exercised: the air common to men who live on the vices, the follies, or the baser fears of mankind; the air of moral nihilism common to keepers of gambling hells and disorderly houses.'

This then, this fat, disreputable idler, was the individual into whose keeping the care and happiness of a wife, her mother and her weak-minded brother had been consigned by destiny. And for seven years, strange as it may sound, all went smoothly and, on the surface, harmoniously. Both wife and mother had a compelling passion in common, the welfare of the boy so little able to look after himself; and Verloc, in his easy disregard of everything but himself, his indolent acceptance of things as they were, and his casual generosity, gave them that sense of material security which was their first concern. Their background had been miserable: victims of the inflamed violence of a publican and then, on his decease, struggling to make ends meet by the letting of rooms, they found in the placid stolidity and passive good nature of Verloc, who on his marriage had taken over the whole family, together with the furniture, an absolute haven. The old mother was of the opinion that 'Mr. Verloc was a very nice gentleman,' the brother worshipped him, and as for Winnie Verloc, with her capacity for not looking beneath the surface of things, an attitude adopted to stifle her errant thoughts, she accepted the position without puzzling her head over its implications.

But this happy state of affairs was not ordained to last indefinitely. As readers of *The Secret Agent* are aware, Verloc's settled mode of life was rudely shaken – was, indeed, totally disrupted – by the extremely unpleasant tone adopted by the First Secretary at the foreign Embassy for which he was supposed to work. The old régime had received his alarmist reports on underground plottings with goggle-eyed credulity; but the new régime, as represented by Mr. Vladimir, expressed itself as so sceptical of his usefulness that he was threatened, in crude but precise language, with being dropped altogether unless he could accomplish something definite, something to arouse public opinion against the menace of subversive activities, and accomplish it quickly.

But when we first see Verloc he is walking tranquilly towards the Embassy for this interview. Being content, as I have said, with things as they were, 'he surveyed through the park railings the evidences of the town's opulence and luxury with an approving eye. All these people had to be protected.' Without being respectable he had, we are told, a feeling for respectability, for we must remember that he was in the pay of a capitalist government and, naturally enough, wanted this agreeable source of income to continue. And behind that, perhaps hardly recognised, the meeting on which he was bent – a meeting that, if known, would have given his anarchist associates a horrible eye-opener – may have induced in him a need for self-justification. Even a Verloc, free of vulgar prejudices as he may believe himself to be, scarcely relishes the idea of being charged with treachery.

He had gone to the appointment with a certain justified jauntiness, but he came away from it not in a chastened mood, but seething with indignation and dull ferocity. Above all, he came away from it a very frightened man. His bluff had been called and his impudent efforts to defend himself had been curtly brushed aside. Instead of being regarded as a defender of society, which had been his pose for years, he was now regarded as a brazen fake, and the whole edifice he had constructed was reeling beneath him. For he was faced by the dismal alternative of blowing up Greenwich Observatory or of losing his job.

It was typical of Verloc's mentality that the deeper he sunk in trouble, the more he retired into himself, and that it was only when he was cornered, finally and officially, by the logic of facts that he flung everything to the winds. It was not alone that he was terrified of being exposed to his anarchist comrades, not alone that he had never confided in his wife, of whom he was selfishly fond 'with the regard one has for one's chief possession,' but that his mind was naturally tortuous. Even if there had been no ostensible reason for his leading a double life, he would probably have led one instinctively, and his reticence was a safeguard which had become second nature, particularly as it suited his native lethargy not even to talk, much less think, more than was necessary.

This does not imply that he did not brood over his worries, but his brooding went round in a circle and he had not the wit to perceive that once the foreign Embassy had changed their tone, he would never again be safe with them. But perhaps, with his love of easily earned money, he could not bring himself even to contemplate such a disaster. No wonder he returned from the Continent, whither he had gone in the vain hope of finding someone to do the deed, with, in Conrad's delicious phrase, 'a mind evidently unrefreshed by the wonders of foreign travel and a countenance unlighted by the joys of home-coming.' The awful problem was still unsolved, time was running short, and where the devil could he turn?

It was then, in the pitiable irony of things, that Winnie Verloc all unconsciously told him in so many words what he could do. Fearful lest her husband should grow weary of supporting her brother – her heroic old mother, having the same haunting fear, had recently departed to an almshouse, so that part of the burden, at least, should be lifted – she had constantly instilled into Stevie's receptive, limited mind the idea that Verloc was a paragon of all the virtues. He proved only too apt a pupil, and

Winnie, observing the alacrity with which he tried to forestall Verloc's slightest wish in his dog-like devotion, sought to strengthen Stevie's dependent position by drawing her husband's attention to his eager helpfulness. In her solicitude for her afflicted brother, which had a quality of passionate maternalism, she uttered the fatal words, 'You could do anything with that boy, Adolf. . . . . . He would go through fire for you.' Thus was born the germ of Verloc's scheme, which was to work on Stevie's well-known hatred of cruelty to such a pitch, that, in an ecstacy of humanitarianism, he would plant the bomb as a gesture against injustice. In that guileless heart, incapable of taking in more than one impression at a time, anything that the admired Mr. Verloc asked him to do would be right.

It is only fair to Verloc to say that he had no expectation of any harm happening to the lad. But it might be added that it never entered his head to plant the bomb himself, though if Stevie was to emerge scatheless and undetected, why not he? And it might also be added that even if Stevie *were* caught, his notorious, dumb stubbornness when, to his clouded intelligence, such stubbornness was in a good cause, would save Verloc's own invaluable self from the attentions of the police. And anyhow the boy's obvious feeble-mindedness would prevent him getting into any very great trouble. It is not suggested that Verloc's arrangement for Stevie to stay for some short time previously with Michaelis, the ex-convict who had served a long sentence for involvement in a shooting affray and whose cottage was near the scene of action, was part of his calculation, but the idea cannot be summarily dismissed. Verloc was up to anything, and the 'moral nihilism,' of which Conrad wrote, was in full possession of his being.

But if Verloc could act thus merely in fear of what might

happen to him, his behaviour after the death of his brother-in-law and his abject, full confession to the Assistant Commissioner of Police prove the total and ineradicable nature of his frantic concern for himself. Certainly, he was sorry about Stevie and attempted to comfort his wife in general terms which sounded rather like a conventional letter of condolence from a semi-stranger – and how could it be otherwise when it was *his* sufferings and worries that really mattered! – but her icy silence, which concealed the maddened raging of her heart, nonplussed him and he began to lose patience. He still cherished the illusion that he was loved for himself, and he played his master card by remarking, 'Do be reasonable, Winnie. What would it have been if you had lost me?' Lost him whom she had married so that Stevie could be safe, lost him who had murdered her beloved brother!

The end of Verloc was so appalling in his sudden realisation that his wife had gone insane and meant to kill him, that it ought perhaps to arouse some sort of pity, if only the shocked, impersonal pity one feels for the victim of any murder; but though it was dreadful enough in all conscience, it is difficult to summon up even a breath of that emotion. The wretched Verloc was simply not worth it! And yet, and yet – listen to this: 'He was lying on his back and staring upwards. He saw partly on the ceiling and partly on the wall the moving shadow of an arm with a clenched hand holding a carving knife. It flickered up and down. Its movements were leisurely. They were leisurely enough for Mr. Verloc to recognise the limb and the weapon. They were leisurely enough for him to take in the full meaning of the portent, and to taste the flavour of death rising in his gorge. His wife had gone raving mad – murdering mad. They were leisurely enough for the first paralysing effect of this discovery to pass away before a resolute determination to come out victorious from the ghastly struggle with that armed lunatic. They were leisurely enough for Mr. Verloc to elaborate a plan of defence involving a dash behind the table, and the felling of the woman to the ground with a heavy wooden chair. But they were not leisurely enough to allow Mr. Verloc the time to move either hand or foot. The knife was already planted in his breast. It met no resistance on its way. Hazard has such accuracies ...... Mr. Verloc, the Secret Agent, turning slightly on his side with the force of the blow, expired without stirring a limb, in the muttered sound of the word "Don't" by way of protest.'

So, after all, if it be true that to him who has loved much, much shall be forgiven, then perhaps it is also true that to him who loved himself so much that he lost his life, some measure of pity should be extended.

WINNIE

THERE IS an elemental quality about Winnie Verloc which, suddenly freed of all controls towards the end of the book, was, in the ordinary course of events, unknown even to herself. Her normal behaviour was particularly calm, and she managed her husband, her mother and her brother with a firm tact which kept her little household together in an atmosphere of unruffled content. It is true that, as a child, she had given glimpses of her fiery temperament when, only a small girl, she had 'often faced with blazing eyes the irascible licensed victualler in defence of her brother,' but that 'ardour of protecting compassion,' which was the guiding motive of her existence, had turned into a sleepless, daily vigilance that, being exercised in proportion to her other duties, was as unobtrusive as it was efficient.

She had an instinctive wisdom which purposely excluded from her mind problems she knew she could not solve, and 'steady-eyed like her husband, she preserved an air of unfathomable indifference behind the rampart of the counter' of the little shop by which Verloc purported to make a living. And in the circle of her family, allowing for the difference of the company, she still maintained a quietly dominant manner that, without impinging on any sensibilities, produced a feeling of domestic security which, in its various ways, exactly suited the three people whose lives were, spiritually speaking, dependent upon her.

In certain respects Winnie Verloc was a very simple woman.

Her education had been scanty, she knew nothing and cared nothing about the world at large, and her life was guided by emotions and principles she took for granted and never thought of questioning. She would have been astonished had some one called her self-sacrificing; indeed she would probably have been embarrassed and perhaps even indignant at such words, as being outside the scope of conversation proper to her position as a respectable married woman. And yet she *was* as self-sacrificing as it is possible for a woman to be: she had given up the cherished company of the butcher's son, who could not support them all, for the uncherished company of Verloc, who could; she had made a resolution, costing her tears, not to have children, so that Stevie should never want for her care; and even if she could not restrain the 'faintest possible blush' on thinking of the 'robust' Ossipon, she met his glance with a 'stony face and a faraway gaze.' In brief, she had all the conventions and reticences of her class as it existed some sixty-five years ago, combined with what one can only call a rare sense of abnegation, and was as loyal a wife to the unattractive Verloc as she was a devoted daughter and sister to her two helpless relatives.

And yet, circumscribed as were her days and limited as were her interests, she had, in herself, nothing to do with the grime of Brett Street. There was something about her, something which every reader of the novel must feel, which makes her one of the most moving characters in fiction. For in herself, divorced from her conscious individuality, this 'young woman with a full bust, in a tight bodice, and very broad hips' shed a kind of muted radiance over the sordid surroundings in which she had her being. The local inhabitants did not perceive it, nobody felt magic in the air: all this was reserved for those who hear her story.

It is more than probable that Verloc's lack of small talk and his willingness to let her run the house and its occupants in her own way suited her very well. Her daily round had to be arranged in such a manner as to keep everything going evenly along, giving to the routine a changeless, tranquilising invariability. If she was sparing in her speech, it was not because she was laconic in the absent-minded style of Verloc, bursting with his secrets, but because, in her class, words were used either as a medium for idle gossip, which was not in her line, or were intended to convey messages or to explain actions. Negatively she was not unhappy, as the two people she cared for most were in her charge, while her husband, uncritically good-natured, was frequently absent.

And so the years passed one after the other until that day on which her mother, brooding incessantly on the need to conciliate the excellent Mr. Verloc, took herself off to the almshouse and gave the first real jolt to the secure, if flat, existence under his roof. It may be that this departure, calmly, if rather indignantly, accepted by Winnie, made her less assured of the future, for any upheaval inevitably suggests a new chain of thought, but all she was aware of on her return from the cab drive with her mother was 'an acute pang of loneliness.' This was natural enough, but why, when she informed Verloc that her mother had left them for good, should he have remarked heavily that perhaps it was 'just as well?' Why was it just as well? Why? Is it possible that, at that moment, something unfamiliar and foreboding stirred within her? – 'Mrs. Verloc kept very still, perfectly still, with her eyes fixed in a dreamy, quiet stare. And her heart for the fraction of a second seemed to stand still, too. That night she was "not quite herself," as the saying is, and it was borne upon her with some force that a simple sentence may hold several diverse meanings – mostly disagreeable.' And when, a few minutes later, Verloc announced with his usual unexplanatory husky briefness that he was going to the Continent on the morrow and might be absent for a week or a fortnight, did it add mysteriously to the faint warning atmosphere which seemed to have invaded the room? Certainly, she was 'confirmed in her instinctive conviction that things don't bear looking into very much,' but then, as she probably argued, it had always been like this, and no doubt she automatically banished the thought. And yet, at that instant, all unguessed by her, the whole fabric of her life was beginning to crumble.

Nearly everybody closely concerned knew of the Greenwich explosion before Winnie Verloc, who had been indoors all day and was no reader of newspapers. She was conscious, of course, that something odd was going on in the house on that evening shortly after Verloc's return, what with his queer behaviour and the strange visitors; but she had taught herself to be incurious, and as she believed Stevie to be safe with the kind Michaelis, what had she to worry about? Even when Chief Inspector Heat, exasperated by what he supposed was her evasiveness, told her, without mentioning names, of the bomb tragedy she had no faintest inkling of the truth. ' "I call it silly" she pronounced slowly. She paused. "We ain't downtrodden slaves here." ' Her safe world still walled her in, with all its comforting illusions, and on this occasion there was no warning whisper. Indeed, there was hardly time for any such reaction, for on being shown the tab with the address on it, the tab which, in her sisterly solicitude, she had sewn into her brother's overcoat, a sickening wave of terror replaced almost immediately the amazement with which she had stared at it. The Chief Inspector took the just-arrived Verloc into the inner room, but the distraught woman, distraught with a suddenness and completeness that physically transformed her, 'pressed her ear to the keyhole; her lips were blue, her hands cold as ice, and her pale face, in which the two eyes seemed like two black coals, felt to her as if she were enveloped in flame.'

Even had Verloc been as subtle as he was dense, he could never have guessed what Stevie meant to his sister: he was the very core of her life, the cause of every sacrifice – 'The protection she had extended over her brother had been in its origin of a fierce and indignant complexion. She had to love him with a militant love. She had battled for him – even against herself. His loss had the bitterness of defeat, with the anguish of a baffled passion. It was not an ordinary stroke of death. Moreover, it was not death that took Stevie from her. It was Mr. Verloc who took him away. She had seen him, she had watched him without raising a hand. She had let him go, like – like a fool – a blind fool.'

Winnie Verloc's primitive instincts, which were powerful, lay close to the surface: they had not been toned down by a culture of which she knew nothing, they had been repressed by a sense of protective loyalty. And thus in the backwash of her despair and rage the slate of her past was wiped clean – she was 'a free woman!' But as she gained her freedom, so did she lose her grip on reason. The shock, tearing her from all her moorings, bereaving her of everything she valued most through the cruel treachery of a 'monster,' had been too great. The inhibitions of her life and upbringing slipped from her as though they had never been and, her reeling brain fixed only on immediate revenge, into the plunging blow she aimed at Verloc with the carving knife was put 'all the inheritance of her immemorial and obscure descent, the simple ferocity of the age of caverns, and the unbalanced nervous fury of the age of bar-rooms.'

[123]

These final pages of *The Secret Agent* are among the most tremendous Conrad ever wrote, throwing their tragic mantle over this book with its basically ironic flavour; but though they are almost unbearably dreadful and piteous, there are moments when extreme beauty lays its merciful hand upon them. Could one find more touching words in all Conrad than those in which, describing the profound changes in Winnie under utmost stress, he writes, 'As if the homeless soul of Stevie had flown for shelter straight to the breast of his sister, guardian, and protector, the resemblance of her face with that of her brother grew at every step, even to the droop of the lower lid, even to the slight divergence of the eyes.' And perhaps, indeed, her likeness to Stevie under the overwhelming calamity of his death had brought out an hereditary lack of balance which, in her brother, had always been present; had stirred in her the same primeval urge that, in moments of retributive indignation, hovered close to Stevie. For had not he, agitated by something he had read about a German officer tearing an ear half off a recruit, also seized this same carving knife and, as his sister said, 'would have stuck that officer like a pig had he seen him then.' It would account for much, even possibly for the studied reserve she had invariably and instinctively displayed: she was nearer to Stevie than she herself knew.

The newspaper paragraph which reported her suicide from a Channel steamer that same night spoke of 'this act of madness or despair,' but it was only the climax of a still more appalling act of madness or despair. Her deed had rebounded upon her, not morally but emotionally, and her freedom resembled that of a machine from which the governor has been removed. In her racing, tormented thoughts all her barriers were down, and the last remnants of her servitude, shattered into as many fragments as Stevie's torn body, had fallen from her. Even for Ossipon, whom she met outside the shop and dragged back with her, even for him with whom she had always been so guarded with his 'shameless inviting eyes, whose glance had a corrupt clearness sufficient to enlighten any woman not absolutely imbecile,' she had no longer any reticences. He was her saviour, she would tell him everything, begin at the beginning, *make* him understand! 'Look here, Tom! I was a young girl. I was done up. I was tired. I had two people depending on what I could do, and it did seem as if I couldn't do any more. Two people – mother and the boy. He was much more mine than mother's. I sat up nights and nights with him on my lap, all alone upstairs, when I wasn't more than eight years old myself. And then – he was mine, I tell you – . . . . . . You couldn't understand that. No man can understand it. What was I to do? There was a young fellow – .'

Of all the men in London the unfortunate girl could not have chosen a more worthless confidant than Ossipon. At first, flattered and gratified by her incoherent story, in which, so far as he could make head or tail of it, it appeared that it was Verloc who had been blown up and Verloc's widow who was offering him everything, he had responded with a sort of fraudulent tenderness. But when the truth was at last revealed, when his eyes beheld the murdered Verloc, sheer panic possessed him. He must keep his wits about him, he must pretend to agree, he must get rid of her! Yes, yes, and he must get hold of the money!

A terror of the gallows, an automatic terror stemming from her intense vitality in which the longing to survive had lost all meaning beyond a reflex animal horror of death, had fastened upon Winnie Verloc, and like a woman in delirium (which, of course, she was) she pleaded frantically with Ossipon: 'Don't let them hang me, Tom! Take me out of the country. I'll work for you. I'll slave for you. I'll love you. I've no one in the world.' She might as well have appealed to a deaf mute, for in the soul of the well-known anarchist there was only an urgent desire to be free of her for ever. And, as we know, he did get free of her (in a material sense) by jumping from the train when it had already begun to move, and he did procure the bag containing Verloc's savings.

The final glimpse we have of Winnie is of 'a lady in black with a white face standing in the empty ladies' cabin. The stewardess induced her to lie down there. The lady seemed quite unwilling to speak, and as if she were in some awful trouble.' Later she must have gone on deck, for the stewardess found 'the unhappy lady lying down in one of the hooded seats. Her eyes were open, but she would not answer anything that was said to her.'

Her last fight, the fight against death, ended, as all her other fights had ended, in defeat, but in that defeat there was surely a measure of victory. She had avenged her beloved Stevie, and in a few hours had found the oblivion he had found: they were as much together again as they could ever be.

Although I have been able, by a use of quite remarkable quotations, to suggest some idea of Winnie Verloc, her real essence lies within the novel. But what I have mainly tried to do in these few pages is to denote the harmony of conception which gives such peculiar force to the developed picture of this young woman. As for her reality, the crowning point of characterisation, it is so deeply etched, so beautifully envisaged, that she seems almost to step from the covers in the very hue and pulse of life.

STEVIE

IN A SENSE, one can only look at Stevie from the outside, as the workings of his enfeebled brain cannot satisfactorily be explained by normal psychology. And yet he is so appealing in his helplessness and so vivid to one's perception that he repays some study, particularly as, unlike many weak-minded people, he was naturally kind instead of being naturally malicious. His hatred of cruelty may have been due partly to the brutality he had experienced as a child, but had he not had an unselfish and humane temperament, his reaction might well have taken an entirely different form.

Stevie was easily influenced to admire whole-heartedly or to hate passionately, for if his mind was crippled, his emotions, functioning along a single track, were intense. Any tale of cruelty tended to make him inarticulate, for his visual perception of it far outran his limited vocabulary, and when this happened he seemed to sink back almost into idiocy, squinting, stuttering, repeating, with staccato brevity, such words as 'poor, poor!' or 'bad, bad!' so strongly did his feelings make him aware of his impotence to right the wrong. When, for instance, we see him first he had been listening, with open-mouthed horror, to Karl Yundt, that 'disgusting old man,' as Winnie Verloc called him, talking of the rich 'nourishing their greed on the quivering flesh and the warm blood of the people;' and, accepting every word literally, Stevie was found later by Verloc 'gesticulating and murmuring' in the kitchen. His wife had to get out of bed to comfort him and even for her he was far away: 'He glared at me, as if he didn't know who I was, when I went downstairs' she confided to Verloc. 'His heart was going like a hammer.'

But if 'excitement robbed him of his power of connected speech,' in the ordinary way he was as inoffensive as a tame rabbit. Unless thoughts were put into his head, either by sights or words, he had none at all, and his spare time was 'occupied by drawing circles with compass and pencil on a piece of paper. He applied himself to that pastime with great industry, with his elbows spread out and bowed low over the kitchen table.' Being vacuous in himself but having, when agitated, the emotions of an angry saint, he existed only as a vegetable or a dynamo, depending completely on whether his blinkered conception soothed or disturbed him. And thus, as he could seldom explain anything, he was incalculable beyond a certain point.

Although Stevie 'helped his sister with blind love and docility in her household duties' and although she understood him better than anybody else did, there were moments when his sense of loyalty to some one who had aroused his compassion made him so stubborn and secretive that even she was out of her depth. The incident when, as an office-boy, he had alarmed the whole building where he was employed by letting off fireworks on the staircase because 'two other office-boys had worked upon his feelings by tales of injustice and oppression' remained obscure in its pointlessness, and it was 'only later that Winnie obtained from him a misty and confused confession.' Being much simpler than a normal person, he could, at times, appear much more complex, for as his mental processes did not function according to the general pattern, he could not express himself coherently and, in every queer thing he did, was utterly unself-seeking.

And it was on the recognised traits of his character – indignant pity, staunch devotion, secretive loyalty, and incapacity to grasp more than one point at a time – that Verloc worked to such a pitch that he became his willing tool to execute his plan for the blowing up of Greenwich Observatory. As we know, Winnie Verloc had ceaselessly drilled into him that Verloc was the best of men, and Stevie, being receptive to such impressions, came to believe that this was actually true – especially, no doubt, as Verloc, unlike his father, neither beat him nor cursed him. As Conrad writes, 'His father's anger, the irritability of gentlemen lodgers, and Mr. Verloc's predisposition to immoderate grief' – a grief invented by Winnie to keep her brother quiet – 'had been the main sanctions of Stevie's self-restraint. Of these sentiments, all easily provoked, but not always easy to understand, the last had the greatest moral efficiency – because Mr. Verloc was *good.*' (How wonderfully the underlining of 'good' gives us an insight into the workings of Stevie's stunted and yet sensitive brain. In the world there were good and evil, no half-measures, no fine lines of distinction; and Mr. Verloc, quite oblivious to the fact, stood at the very summit, the underlined summit, of what was good in mankind.)

In the usual way, Verloc 'extended as much recognition to Stevie as a man not particularly fond of animals may give to his wife's beloved cat; and this recognition, benevolent and per-functory, was essentially of the same quality.' It was his wife's calculated habit of frequently drawing her husband's attention to Stevie's exalted regard for him, and his own sluggishly awakened observation of the lad's eager desire to do his slightest bidding, that, as I have said before, gave Verloc the idea of using him to solve his troubles. But there was something more. Single-minded devotion was all very well, but for the enterprise Verloc had in view a quality was called for which he himself did not possess, and this was the quality of fanatical resolution. And, as Conrad comments, 'though not much of a psychologist, Mr. Verloc had gauged the depth of Stevie's fanaticism.'

But first of all, Stevie had to be convinced that what he would be called upon to do was right, for having had a belief in law and order impressed firmly on him, he would rather have been torn apart by wild horses than disobey the dictates of his conscience. And therefore, with his rooted code, he must be made to see that what would once have appeared wrong was now right. Here fate played one of its terrible tricks on Winnie Verloc. On that drive to the almshouse with his mother and sister, the wretched state both of the cabman and his horse had aroused in Stevie such an overwhelming wave of pity that his 'tenderness to all pain and all misery, the desire to make the horse happy and the driver happy, had reached the point of a bizarre longing to take them to bed with him.' So being unable to help them himself, Stevie's troubled mind turned instinctively to the police, of whom he had 'an ideal conception . . . . . . as a sort of benevolent institution for the suppression of evil.' But when, on uttering the word 'Police' to his sister, she informed him, as a pacifying crumb of philosophy, that the police could do nothing about it, she planted in his guileless heart the first germ of doubt of their universal power and benignity. Presently she added, to stop his persistence, 'Don't you know what the police are for, Stevie? They are there so that them as have nothing shouldn't take anything away from them who have.' It was neither a cynical nor an indignant remark, it was merely explanatory, and intended, as so many of her words to Stevie, to keep him from fruitless worrying; but it had a very different effect: Stevie's trust had been undermined. And therefore when

Verloc on his walks with his brother-in-law, prior to broaching the real purpose, 'modified Stevie's view of the police by conversations full of subtle reasonings,' it is not to be wondered that 'never had a sage more attentive and admiring audience,' for it already *had* been modified.

It had been Winnie's own idea that Stevie, fretting in the absence of his mother, should accompany her husband on his walks, and so once again, in the most cunningly natural manner, fate lay in wait for Stevie's sister and, while seeming to play into her hands, was stealthily removing the last safeguards. She was so pleased with the result of her plan and would watch with such contentment the 'two figures down the squalid street, one tall and burly, the other slight and short, with a thin neck, and the peaked shoulders raised slightly under the large semi-transparent ears,' that she was even once led to murmur, 'Might be father and son.'

When Stevie was affected by the story of some abominable wrong 'the anguish of immoderate compassion was succeeded by the pain of an innocent but pitiless rage,' and this is what had happened now: Verloc's arguments had been very convincing. But Winnie, noting that he 'moped no longer at the foot of the clock, but muttered to himself in corners in a threatening tone,' put it down to his hearing too much on these walks, during which Verloc, in pursuit of his avocation, 'met and conversed with various persons;' and she was delighted therefore when her husband suggested that perhaps a few days with Michaelis, living his ascetic life in a cottage near Greenwich Common, would be good for the boy. (Fate was still on her track.) As for Stevie, he 'offered no objection. He seemed rather eager, in a bewildered sort of way . . . . . . His expression was proud, apprehensive, and concentrated, like that of a small child en-

trusted for the first time with a box of matches and the permission to strike a light.' Winnie had not noticed this, as such glances
were reserved for Verloc; but when, at the instant of departure,
she begged her brother not to get his clothes dirty in the country
and he gave her a look which 'for the first time in his life seemed
to lack the quality of perfect childlike trustfulness. It was haugh-
tily gloomy,' she was amused at his apparently taking offence,
for he was notoriously untidy and must constantly have been
warned. But could she have looked into his heart, she would not
have smiled, she would have screamed aloud. And so, under her
equable gaze, he passed down the street on his errand of justice
and humanity – passed, like a martyr of old, to his lamentable
death in the full belief of a glorious mission.

It was an extraordinary feat of imagination to have created
such a figure as Stevie who, intellectually a half-wit, not only
arouses our sympathy, but interests us as a human being. And to
have maintained the same level throughout, never exaggerating
or underestimating his special niche, as of a person hovering
between two worlds, so that it all rings true to the idea of him
we have formed, was a very great achievement. The secret of
that clouded, compassionate, innocent and dangerous mind may
elude us, but Stevie himself stands out as clearly as the sunlight.

'THE PROFESSOR'

OF THE FOUR ANARCHISTS in *The Secret Agent*, each indelibly individualised, only one, the man called the Professor, is worth much attention psychologically. As regards the others, the ex-convict Michaelis, who had been mixed up in the accidental shooting of a policeman which made him 'miserable at heart,' was a gentle dreamer, subsisting on a diet of raw carrots, dry bread and milk, who believed that the possession of private property would inevitably come to an end 'by the mere development of its inherent viciousness;' old Karl Yundt, with his 'extraordinary expression of underhand malevolence,' was a half-extinct volcano mouthing imprecations against society, who had been, according to the Professor, 'a posturing shadow all his life;' and the young and lusty Ossipon was, despite his authorship of a 'popular quasi-medical study (in the form of a pamphlet promptly seized by the police) entitled "The Corroding Vices of the Middle Classes," ' a vicious and cowardly rogue himself, living on the savings of stupid girls and, as we know, not above stealing the Verloc money and abandoning Winnie Verloc to her fate.

But the Professor was a very different type – he was dangerous. Conrad writes of him with the same irony, bitter under its playfulness, he applied to Verloc, but he does not deny him character of a sort, the character of a vindictive, narrow-minded, insufferable fanatic who, miserably stunted and poverty-stricken, was yet quite prepared to go short of food in order to

purchase explosives and quite ready to live entirely by himself
in a bare room in the conviction of his own boundless superiority.

'His parentage' says Conrad 'was obscure, and he was generally known by his nickname of Professor. His title to that desig-
nation consisted in his having been once assistant demonstrator
in chemistry at some technical institute. He quarrelled with the
authorities upon a question of unfair treatment. Afterwards he
obtained a post in the laboratory of a manufactory of dyes.
There, too, he had been treated with revolting injustice. His
struggles, his privations, his hard work to raise himself in the
social scale, had filled him with such an exalted conviction of his
own merit that it was extremely difficult for the world to treat
him with justice.'

But it is obvious that, however the Professor had been treated,
he would have come out in his true colours sooner or later. For
he was one of those misfits who considered everybody else a
misfit and whose resolve to scourge humanity, founded upon
megalomania in contemplation of his grievances, had reached
a pitch where its moral purpose had become so subordinated to
his hatred of mankind that universal destruction was now
his real aim. As he explained to Ossipon, 'First the great multitude of the weak must go, then the only relatively strong. You
see? First the blind, then the deaf and the dumb, then the halt
and the lame – and so on. Every taint, every vice, every preju-
dice, every convention must meet its doom.' And when Ossipon,
to whom such views were distasteful, perhaps because he guessed
that he would be one of the first to be destroyed, asked nervously
who then would remain, the Professor replied with his usual
dogmatic assertiveness, 'I remain – if I am strong enough' –
surely rather a modest proviso for the Professor to make!

In manner he was self-assured, impervious to argument, and

scornfully oblivious of the comforts of life except for an occasional glass of beer at the Silenus. It is probable that this portentous self-assurance was partly, at least, due to his wretched and repellent appearance, a kind of protection he had instinctively adopted, for no one more outwardly insignificant ever breathed, as may be judged from Conrad's description – 'The flat cheeks, of a greasy, unhealthy complexion, were merely smudged by the miserable quality of a thin dark whisker. The lamentable inferiority of the whole physique was made ludicrous by the supremely self-confident bearing of the individual. His speech was curt, and he had a particularly impressive manner of keeping silent.'

But he was not a poseur like Karl Yundt, he was a man of action. How many bombs, apart from the fatal one he had prepared at Verloc's bidding, he had handed out to whomsoever asked for them, who can tell? But many or few, his fixation had formidable possibilities and, given the opportunity, he would willingly have wrecked the universe. He always carried on his person not only the means of killing himself but the means of killing any policeman who might try to arrest him, and he would not have hesitated to use them. Therein lay the sense of power which sweetened his arid days. The 'bespectacled, dingy little man' intimidated the large Ossipon, not so much because of the explosive he carried, but because of his character, just as a child may dominate an elephant despite its size and its tusks.

And yet, for all his assurance, the Professor did not really understand himself. If his truculence of manner resulted partly from his weedy dwarfishness, and his theory of destruction partly from the wrongs he had suffered, he was also, by his very nature, an evil man attempting to justify himself – 'The Professor's indignation found in itself a final cause that absolved him from the sin of turning to destruction as the agent of his ambition. To destroy public faith in legality was the imperfect formula of his pedantic fanaticism . . . . . . He was a moral agent – that was settled in his mind. By exercising the agency with ruthless defiance he procured for himself the appearances of power and personal prestige. It pacified his unrest.'

And thus, despite his arrogant tone, his attitude was tinged by motives that were commonplace, petty and sordid. Revenge and vanity interpenetrated his being, and though he was not interested in self-analysis, which he would probably have regarded as a symptom of mawkish degeneracy, he was profoundly conscious of his own splendid isolation. Having long since determined finally every question that required answering, he was now, from his pinnacle, concerned only with the science of destruction. In his utter contempt for others, he even allowed himself occasionally the grim relaxation of joking, in a one-sided manner, with such a worm as Ossipon. When, for instance, the latter, learning, as he supposed, that Verloc had been blown up, which meant that the attractive Mrs. Verloc (who would now own the shop) was a widow, mused aloud in the presence of the Professor, 'I wonder what I had better do now?', back came the answer in a flash, 'Fasten yourself upon the woman for all she's worth.' Thus did the Professor reveal his sense of humour, his knowledge of Ossipon and, incidentally, his lack of compassion or decency.

It might be argued that, endowed with the optimism of complete certitude, the Professor should have been a happy man, but this was not altogether true. His peace of mind was haunted by the existence of such countless masses of people, and 'the thought of a mankind as numerous as the sands of the seashore, as indestructible, as difficult to handle, oppressed him.' How could even he, faced by such odds, 'turn the world into a shambles,' and what could be done with their 'unattackable stolidity?' Every pioneer is almost certain to have moments, if not of doubt, at least of despondency, when he considers the dense unreceptiveness of humanity; but if the Professor was no exception to this rule, which for him had its special application, it was only intermittently that he allowed himself to feel despondent. He was built of firmer stuff, and in the very last sentences of *The Secret Agent* he shows himself as assured as ever, even if, on his walk, he did have to avert his eyes from 'the odious multitude of mankind' – 'He had no future. He disdained it. He was a force. His thoughts caressed the images of ruin and destruction. He walked frail, insignificant, shabby, miserable – and terrible in the simplicity of his idea calling madness and despair to the regeneration of the world. Nobody looked at him. He passed on unsuspected and deadly, like a pest in the street full of men.'

TWO POLICEMEN

BOTH the Assistant Commissioner of Police (we are not told his name) and Chief Inspector Heat of the Special Crimes branch are interesting in themselves, the first as an individual and the second as a type, but their chief interest for readers of *The Secret Agent* lies in the clash of their personalities and points of view. They were equally concerned to unravel the mystery which surrounded the Greenwich explosion, but whereas the Assistant Commissioner approached the problem from what one might call a psychological angle, the Chief Inspector approached it from what one might call a Department angle. Men of integrity in their different ways, they distrusted one another, largely because of their disparate qualities and diverse sense of values.

The Assistant Commissioner, who had recently returned from a tropical colony where he had successfully exercised his police powers untrammelled, 'did not like the work he had to do now. He felt himself dependent on too many subordinates and too many masters. The near presence of that strange emotional phenomenon called public opinion weighed upon his spirits, and alarmed him by its irrational nature;' while the Chief Inspector felt that the newcomer was an upstart who wanted to interfere too much with the established and efficient routine of police procedure and investigation. At their interview in the office of the Assistant Commissioner, the Chief Inspector even tried to fence with his superior, and had not the other, who was nobody's fool, guessed that he was being disingenuous, he would not have revealed the vital clue he had come upon – the patch of cloth bearing Stevie's address on the collar of his overcoat.

And he would have acted so not from inimical personal reasons, but because he was convinced that he alone could deal with the evidence in the correct manner, without having to disclose the fact of Verloc's existence and all the knowledge he had gained from his acquaintanceship, unofficial in a manner of speaking, with that shady character. The well-known police phrase 'from information received' appealed, beyond doubt, to the Chief Inspector, who had learnt the importance of the devious in the search for proof. But when, cornered by the astuteness of the Assistant Commissioner, he resolved, with a sudden change of front, to tell him what he knew, or as much of it as was forced from him, the contemptuous thought, 'a fool and his job are soon parted,' flashed through his head; though it was 'immediately followed by the sober reflection that a higher official, even when "fired out" (this was the precise image), has still the time as he flies through the door to launch a nasty kick at the shinbones of a subordinate.' Thus he had no choice but to take the plunge, and very soon the Assistant Commissioner, with his promptings, knew all about Verloc and the house in Brett Street.

The Chief Inspector, arguing along conveniently conventional lines, thought that it would be an excellent preliminary step to have Michaelis, living but three miles from the scene of the explosion, put under arrest, even though he was positive that he knew much less about it 'than certain individuals he had in his mind, but whose arrest seemed to him inexpedient, besides being a more complicated matter, on account of the rules of the game. The rules of the game did not protect so much Michaelis, who was an ex-convict. It would be stupid not to take advantage of legal facilities.' Even on being informed by the Assistant Commissioner that full evidence would be required, he saw no reason to hint at other possibilities, but answered with 'virtuous complacency' that there would be 'no difficulty in getting up sufficient evidence against *him.*'

This has an unpleasant ring, but Heat was an 'old department hand' and had his own ideas as to how to ferret out the facts of a case. He did believe that Michaelis was involved to some extent, and his arrest, justified in any event, would give him time, as he presumably argued, to look further into the matter. But motives being seldom simple, there were still other thoughts in his head: to begin with, he did not want to disclose the existence of Verloc, so useful as a police informer; and secondly, 'deep down in his blameless bosom of an average married citizen, almost unconscious but potent nevertheless, the dislike of being compelled by events to meddle with the desperate ferocity of the Professor had its say . . . . . . Not that the Chief Inspector was afraid of him; on the contrary, he meant to have him some day. But not yet: he meant to get hold of him in his own time, properly and effectively, according to the rules of the game. The present was not the right time for attempting that feat, not the right time for many reasons personal and of public service.'

If the accumulated evidence, as he probably expected, finally led to the Professor, then he would not have hesitated to tackle him, for his reputation for courage was well-founded; but meanwhile he had Michaelis, a notorious ticket-of-leave ex-convict, to throw to the public. It was a first move, which he hoped might be the last, but his mind was not closed. With ordinary criminals, among whom his work formerly lay, the Chief Inspector had been regarded as a fair man, but then he considered them as human beings, whereas for anarchists he had nothing but a 'hard, merciless contempt.' And though in any circumstances he was, in essence, a just man, there were degrees within which he exercised this virtue, and he was glad of the loopholes it offered. As he remarked to the Assistant Commissioner, such a man as Michaelis, with the record he had, had 'no business to be at large anyhow.'

But if the Chief Inspector was anxious to have Michaelis arrested, the Assistant Commissioner was anxious not to have him arrested. To start with (which was, of course, the main point), he did not believe that he was implicated, though naturally this would have to be looked into; but furthermore he too, like his assistant, had a private reason. The Great Lady who, as his wife's patroness, had also befriended him, was, in the independent-mindedness of her aristocratic background, openly befriending the ex-convict – it was actually in a cottage belonging to her that he was happily rusticating in the country – and it was manifest that she would hold it violently against him if the saint-like Michaelis should again be seized by the police. It was a worrying situation, and he 'made a reflection extremely unbecoming his official position without being really creditable to his humanity: "If the fellow is laid hold of again," he thought, "she will never forgive me." '

And yet both men were acting according to their codes of duty, even if other influences helped, more or less subconsciously, to reinforce these codes. The Assistant Commissioner, a fastidious-minded man of few illusions, was infinitely more sensitive than the Chief Inspector; but neither would have allowed any personal consideration, whether subtle or concrete and however awkward it might turn out to be, to stand between him and his duty unless he had, mentally, been able to strengthen his decision by arguments that, not appearing to affect his judgment, being either outside his official attitude or proper to his official attitude, nevertheless gave to his decision a sort of slightly dogmatic assertiveness. We are all probably rather like that, but not having a Conrad for our biographer we mostly escape the revelation.

Even had no such case as the Greenwich explosion arisen, even had their relationship always been easy within its set limits, it is clear that the Chief Inspector would never have understood the Assistant Commissioner who, with his questing scepticism, would inevitably have seemed to him queer. But having a certain tolerance under his veiled distrust, Heat had hitherto regarded his superior as being 'in the main harmless – odd-looking but harmless.' He was the third Assistant Commissioner under whom he had served, and he had doubtless considered them all as quite unnecessary, men temporarily placed over him because of political or social influence, ornamental nonentities to be tactfully handled just as long as they did not really interfere with his work, which was the one thing that mattered.

But when he perceived that the Assistant Commissioner was not satisfied with his handling of the affair and that he was, as he told himself, practically 'chucked out of the case,' mild disapproval gave way to extreme and virtuous disgust and he suddenly resolved that, as a private citizen, he would call on Verloc that same evening on the chance that a talk with him, now known to be the 'other man,' might 'be of a nature to incriminate Michaelis. It was a conscientiously professional hope in the main, but not without its moral value,' for obviously if this hope were justified, not only would he rehabilitate himself with his superior, which would be a barbed feather in his cap, but he might be saved trouble in various ways.

Imagine his feelings therefore when, arriving at the house in

Brett Street, he learnt that the Assistant Commissioner had been there before him and had already had a long conversation with Verloc. Such was the shock of this discovery, that, only permissible to his code by stretching its implications to the limit if not beyond, he urged the spy to clear out while there was yet time. And even when Verloc, with the lethargic resignation of a ruined gambler, announced his intention of making a complete breast of everything, he still urged him to get away. True, he was sure that if Verloc were to speak out fully it would 'disorganise the whole system of supervision,' but when he joined to this the thought that 'it would leave Michaelis unscathed; it would drag to light the Professor's home industry,' the man of justice and courage had, in the cataclysm of the moment, melted into the schemer who *must* carry things out by his own tried methods. In due course he would doubtless have recovered his sense of proportion and his instinctive fairness, but meanwhile he felt almost as baffled as the wretched Verloc. He, Chief Inspector Heat, owed a duty to society, and how could he fulfil this duty if he was to be thwarted at every turn! But just as he was deeply perturbed, professionally, morally and personally, by the behaviour of his immediate superior, which could only lead to chaos, so was his immediate superior deeply dissatisfied and annoyed by the system which, to the Chief Inspector, was so all-essential. For a year and a half he had 'concealed his irritation with the system and the subordinates in his office. A square peg forced into a round hole, he had felt like a daily outrage that long-established smooth roundness into which a man of less sharply angular shape would have fitted himself, with voluptuous acquiescence, after a shrug or two. What he resented most was just the necessity of taking so much on trust.'

The two men were inherently at loggerheads, but although the Assistant Commissioner appreciated Heat's good points as well as his bad, the appreciation was not mutual. Indeed, it may be questioned whether the Chief Inspector considered that an Assistant Commissioner should possess any points at all, or any precise views, where crime detection was concerned: all that ought to be left to the experts such as himself. And yet, self-assured as he was, to some extent he may have been the victim of his superior's detestation of his job. The truth is, the Assistant Commissioner had never wanted to abandon his work in the tropical colony, but having married impulsively during one of his leaves, only to discover that his wife, whose main preoccupations were social, flatly declined to accompany him abroad, he had had to throw up his post there and accept this very unwelcome substitute. In such a jaundiced frame of mind it would perhaps always have been difficult to satisfy him, but when to this was added the fact that he did really think the system to be wrong, it was almost inevitable that Heat, one of its principal protagonists, should be regarded with especial disfavour, in so far as his native balance and uprightness allowed him to be personally biased.

There are more important figures in *The Secret Agent* than either of these policemen I have been discussing, but all the same their reactions upon one another, taken in conjunction with the secret influences that swayed their attitude, make them a very interesting study.

4

UNDER WESTERN EYES

1910

RAZUMOV

To understand Razumov in general terms we must appreciate that the future he originally visualised for himself was the perfectly normal one of obtaining, entirely through his own merits, a good administrative appointment. Having no relations – he was the illegitimate son of an archpriest's daughter, now dead, and of an aristocratic prince, who helped him financially but whom he had met only once for a few unrevealing minutes at a lawyer's office – not being interested in politics beyond expressing a vague liberalism, and mixing relatively little with his fellow-students, he led a particularly solitary life. When the book opens all his energies are concentrated on winning the silver medal presented by the Ministry of Education, for if he were to succeed in this his career would be virtually assured.

He was a 'tall, well-proportioned young man, quite unusually dark for a Russian from the Central Provinces. His good looks would have been unquestionable if it had not been for a peculiar lack of fineness in his features . . . . . . His manner, too, was good . . . . . . With his younger compatriots he took the attitude of an inscrutable listener, a listener of the kind that hears you out intelligently and then – just changes the subject. This sort of trick . . . . . . procured for Mr. Razumov a reputation of profundity. Amongst a lot of exuberant talkers, in the habit of exhausting themselves daily by ardent discussion, a comparatively taciturn personality is naturally credited with reserve power......This, in a country where an opinion may be a legal crime visited by death or sometimes by a fate worse than death, meant that he was worthy of being trusted with forbidden opinions.'

It was this reputation, together with his 'quiet readiness to oblige his comrades even at the cost of personal inconvenience,' which induced the rabid, simple Haldin to seek his help after he had thrown his bomb at Mr. de P—. He believed that Razumov was an exalted spirit who would understand and sympathise, whereas, in reality, he could not have chosen, for confidant, a man more bitterly opposed to violence and everything it stood for. His view was both philosophic and personal, and, as was only natural, the instant he found himself compromised by Haldin's presence and his whole future imperilled, his opposition became infinitely intensified. He 'saw himself shut up in a fortress, worried, badgered, perhaps ill-used. He saw himself deported by an administrative order, his life broken, ruined, and robbed of all hope. He saw himself – at best – leading a miserable existence under police supervision, in some small, far-away provincial town, without friends to assist his necessities or even take any steps to alleviate his lot.'

In fact, he saw nothing but ruin ahead, a ruin thrust upon him for no reason at all; and if he consented, as he did, to do what Haldin begged him to do, get hold of a peasant called Ziemianitch, who might, with his horses and sledge, manage to smuggle him out of St. Petersburg, it was mainly through an urgent desire to be rid of him immediately and for ever. Unfortunately the wretched Ziemianitch was lying dead drunk on a heap of straw, and it was impossible, even by a thrashing, to awake him. What on earth was left! Razumov felt the inertia of despair: 'Between the two he was done for. Between the drunkenness of the peasant incapable of action and the dream-intoxication of the idealist incapable of perceiving the reason of things, and the true character of men.' He hated Haldin with an overwhelming hate, but he had to justify to himself his hardening thoughts: 'Do I want his death? No! I would save him if I could – but no one can do that – he is the withered member which must be cut off. If I must perish through him, let me at least not perish with him, and associated against my will with his sombre folly that understands nothing either of men or things.' And again, 'What is he with his indignation, with his talk of bondage – with his talk of God's justice? All that means disruption. Better that thousands should suffer than that a people should become a dis-integrated mass, helpless like dust in the wind. Obscurantism is better than the light of incendiary torches . . . . . . And am I, who love my country – and have nothing but that to love and put my faith in – am I to have my future, perhaps my usefulness, ruined by this sanguinary fanatic?'

He was working himself up to a drastic decision: 'Betray. A great word. What is betrayal? They talk of a man betraying his country, his friends, his sweetheart. There must be a moral bond first. All a man can betray is his conscience. And how is my conscience engaged here; by what bond of common faith, of common conviction, am I obliged to let that fanatical idiot drag me down with him? On the contrary – every obligation of true courage is the other way.'

As long as there was a chance of getting hold of Ziemianitch he still had the faint hope that, once Haldin had disappeared, he might conceivably avoid being implicated. But now he was *bound* to be implicated, unless he were forthwith to take so dramatic and determined a step that he positively could not be suspected. But, of course, he had again to rationalise his decision and convince himself that what he was about to do – betray Haldin to the authorities – was what he ought to do. He genuinely did feel that Haldin was a murderer, a menace who should be eliminated, but his fury against him, though not simulated, was heightened by his own position, forced on him by this criminal maniac, and by his urgent longing to clear his name and continue his chosen work.

But the actual betrayal, if successful from one angle, did not help. Incalculable complications followed in its wake, and though his physical safety and position were momentarily assured, everything else was turned upside down, and his student's career was for ever wrecked, not so much by the police, although he was 'always being made to feel that he had committed himself,' as by his own tormented unrest. The process by which, caught up in the network of an unknown stratum in which all his aspirations, everything he had planned to accomplish, seemed hopeless of attainment, he was led finally to espionage for the Government, is told, in so far as it need be told, in my section on Councillor Mikulin; but it cannot too strongly be stressed that, not only had his past experience increased his horror of illegal activities, but that it altered him almost beyond recognition by bringing out all sorts of things in himself of whose very existence he must have been totally unaware.

Of course, anybody thrown off his balance by a sudden, unexpected and disastrous blow of fate is liable to exhibit traits foreign to his usual mode of thought and outside his normal line of behaviour, and Razumov was no exception to this rule. But perhaps, because the ruin of his hopes was so total, mingled with his Russian fatalistic extremism, his collapse took a form which, in its more extravagant manifestations, would appear to an Occidental mind at once grotesque and disgraceful. For example, when he was about to leave Russia for Switzerland he permitted his fellow-student, and ardent admirer, Kostia, to steal money from his father in order to provide him with funds; but on his journey he threw the unopened package of notes out of the window, explaining the whole thing later in these words from his diary: 'He was a fool, but not a thief. I made him one. It was necessary. I had to confirm myself in my contempt and hate for what I had betrayed. I have suffered from as many vipers in my heart as any social democrat of them all – vanity, ambitions, jealousies, shameful desires, evil passions of envy and revenge. I had my security stolen from me, years of good work, my best hopes.'

This diary of his was a sort of unbaring of his soul (a very reckless expedient), ultimately intended for Nathalie Haldin, and he went on to say, 'Listen – now comes the real confession. The other was nothing. To save me, your trustful eyes had to entice my thoughts to the very edge of the blackest treachery. I could see them constantly looking at me with the confidence of your pure heart which had not been touched by evil things. Victor Haldin had stolen the truth of my life from me, who had nothing else in the world, and he boasted of living on through you on this earth where I had no place to lay my head. She will marry some day, he had said – and your eyes were trustful. And do you know what I said to myself? I shall steal his sister's soul from her. When we met that first morning in the gardens, and you spoke to me confidingly in the generosity of your spirit, I was thinking, "Yes, he himself by talking of her trustful eyes has delivered her into my hands!" If you could have looked into my heart, you would have cried out aloud with terror and disgust' – and more to the same repellent and raving effect.

Both these confessions are, of course, scandalous, but the

point I wish to make is that they were completely alien to the balanced attitude of this sober-minded young man, and that his legitimate sense of indignation had stirred up obscure reactions of revenge which, unable to touch the author of his downfall, were intended to injure the innocent so that he himself could obtain a sort of morbid satisfaction in his own hell. A Westerner would, assuredly, have stopped short of staining himself so hopelessly, but the very wildness of these diary entries justifies the truism that nobody knows of what he is capable beyond a certain point.

But it was not only in excessive examples that the change in Razumov was so obvious: 'The choking fumes of falsehood had taken him by the throat – the thought of being condemned to struggle on in that tainted atmosphere without the hope of ever renewing his strength by a breath of fresh air.' He had always been, as we know, a rather solitary man, but that same solitude was peopled by his work and his ambitions, whereas now his solitude, the profound solitude of his inner broodings, was peopled by nightmares: 'The futility of all this overcame him like a curse. Even then he could not believe in the reality of his mission. He looked round despairingly, as if for some way to redeem his existence from that unconquerable feeling.'

But there was no escape, even if he did find a false relief in his diary now that he had met Nathalie Haldin, and a new weight, the weight of remorse mixed with bitter love, had penetrated his soul. His whole existence was a living lie, based upon theories, the outlines of which were losing their validity, and he resembled a tightrope walker trying to perform a feat which, difficult enough at the best of times, had become practically impossible owing to the fact that the rope had begun to sag. In brief, his behaviour had lost its primary motivation, and he drifted about Geneva more like a ghost than like a man determined to impress the enemy by his masterful energy.

It is my opinion that Councillor Mikulin was taking an unjustified risk in presuming that Razumov had the makings of an efficient spy. It is true that, in himself, he was superior to most spies, a different type altogether, and to that extent might be more likely to be trusted; but on the other hand, he was not adaptable enough to sink his personality which, underneath the surface, struggled for utterance. And this was a very grave danger. No doubt he could have carried things off more convincingly had he not met Miss Haldin; but it seems to me that, in any event, he was not cut out for the part, especially as, though inherently a poor actor, he can have been given very little, if any, training. But there again his gaucherie, so crude in its unresponsiveness, might have had the effect of stilling doubts – for how could any spy act in such an ambiguous manner?

Even his haunted appearance was against him, unless we assume that, as one of the supposed attackers of Mr. de P— and as a man ready for anything, he was entitled to look haunted: the reflection of the teacher of languages, 'I could almost feel on me the weight of his unrefreshed, motionless stare, the stare of a man who lies unwinking in the dark, angrily passive in the toils of disastrous thoughts,' must have been universally noticed. On the whole, indeed, it seems rather surprising that, though some of the revolutionists tended to be suspicious, others were sure of him. Thus his uncompromising manner and his sullen expression appear to have worked, for the time being, both ways, and it was only when Sophia Antonovna received from St. Petersburg the news that Ziemianitch, deeply involved, as was supposed, in events subsequent to the assassination, had hanged himself in a fit of remorse, that the genuineness of Razumov was admitted by every one.

And it was then, when 'the only thing to make me safe – a trusted revolutionist for ever' had happened, that, after a brief period of deceptive tranquillity, he knew that he must 'confess, go out – and perish.' Of course this emotion, this change of heart, was due to what Nathalie Haldin had aroused in him; but sooner or later, would it not have happened anyhow in one way or another? Beneath the new and, as it were, dehumanised Razumov, a third Razumov was beginning to stir and can be glimpsed in what he wrote in the later pages of his diary: 'In giving Victor Haldin up, it was myself, after all, whom I have betrayed most basely. You must believe what I say now, you can't refuse to believe this. Most basely. It is through you that I came to feel this so deeply. After all, it is they and not I who have the right on their side! – theirs is the strength of invisible powers. So be it. Only don't be deceived, Natalia Victorovna, I am not converted – and therefore perdition is my lot.'

They were the last words he wrote in his diary, the sheets of which he immediately did up in a parcel and addressed to Miss Haldin. This took place shortly after he made his confession to her.

I have written about this confession when discussing Nathalie Haldin and it is unnecessary to say much concerning it here. But to understand, if only faintly, what he had been through since he met her, I shall quote his words to her just before the shattering truth emerged: 'An hour after I saw you first I knew how it would be. The terrors of remorse, revenge, confession, anger, hate, fear, are like nothing to the atrocious temptation which you put in my way the day you appeared before me with your voice, with your face, in the garden of that accursed villa.' As for the confession itself – 'There is no more to tell . . . . . . It ends here on this very spot.' But if it ruined one life, it cleansed another.

It would be an anti-climax to describe in detail how he then proceeded to confess before an assembled body of the revolutionists; how Nikita (a spy in both camps) deafened him for life by a fearful blow on either ear; how, in his deafness, he was run over by a tramcar and seriously injured; and how, back again in Russia under the care of Tekla, he was cared for in a 'little two-roomed wooden house, in the suburb of some very small town, hiding within the high plank-fence of a yard overgrown with nettles. He was crippled, ill, getting weaker every day, and Tekla the Samaritan tended him unweariedly with the pure joy of unselfish emotion.'

In his Author's Note to *Under Western Eyes* Conrad observes that Razumov was 'an ordinary young man, with a healthy capacity for work and sane ambitions,' and this is an accurate summary of his pre-Haldin character. But lying dormant within him there was something that was not ordinary at all. The conversation he had with Councillor Mikulin, his communings with himself, the diary he kept, show that he had a most unusual mind. But it must be remembered that almost from the beginning of the book we see him under a violent stress, and that such a stress, while it can bewilder a man mentally, may also sharpen his wits. As for his courage, which some readers may be inclined to call in question throughout the Haldin episode, this also was of a very unusual type, for it included, in one gesture, both physical and moral courage – and that is rare. But having confessed to Nathalie, what did he care about the revolutionists! Only a complete confession, at whatever risk, would 'cover up the ignominy of the existence before him.' Indeed, if one were called upon to pronounce a verdict on Razumov, it would be necessary (always allowing for his Russianism which, in a broken man like Razumov, would seem to veer between vileness and self-laceration when it gets the bit in its mouth) to search closely into one's own soul.

NATHALIE HALDIN

THERE IS something particularly straightforward and genuine about Nathalie Haldin which differentiates her at once from most of the characters in *Under Western Eyes*. Living quietly in Geneva with her widowed mother, far from her native Russia where, owing to their openly expressed liberal views, they had been ostracised, she had little practical experience of life; and, as might be expected, being what she was in these circumstances, 'Her glance was as direct and trustful as that of a young man yet unspoiled by the world's wise lessons. And it was intrepid, but in this intrepidity there was nothing aggressive. A naive yet thoughtful assurance is a better definition.'

For all her balance and equability, the English teacher of languages, a friend of both mother and daughter, soon perceived that not only was she fanatically Russian in her sympathies, but was possessed by a sort of Russian mysticism, which was not so much mysticism as the Occidental defines it, but a fundamentally different attitude to existence. As he says, 'I knew her well enough to have discovered her scorn for all the practical forms of political liberty known to the western world. I suppose one must be a Russian to understand Russian simplicity, a terrible corroding simplicity in which mystic phrases clothe a naive and hopeless cynicism. I think sometimes that the psychological secret of the profound difference of that people consists in this, that they detest life, the irremediable life of the earth as it is, whereas we westerners cherish it with perhaps an equal exaggeration of its sentimental value.'

Whether this really describes the Russian outlook or whether it is, rather, a complication on a complication would be hard to say, but there certainly was a directness about Miss Haldin, not affecting her femininity, which seemed to enclose a point of view which found its satisfaction in ideas rather than in facts. In practical life she was sensible, conscientious, dignified and quite astute – for instance, she was not taken in by that eloquent windbag Peter Ivanovitch – but being at heart an idealistic revolutionary, she saw Russia as a unique entity, a land set apart, in which 'the future will be merciful to us all. Revolutionist and reactionary, victim and executioner, betrayer and betrayed, they shall all be pitied together when the light breaks on our black sky at last. Pitied and forgotten; for without that there can be no union and no love.'

In the world of personal affections she was wrapped up, as was Mrs. Haldin, in her brother, whom they both regarded as the noblest of men; and when it was gradually borne in upon them that it was he who had thrown a bomb at the Minister de P—, paying for it with his life, the grief of both women had an intensity beyond tears. Mrs. Haldin retired into a mournful silence which finally destroyed her mind, but Nathalie, displaying another brand of stoicism, maintained an outward calm, a calm necessary for the protection of her mother and witness to her pride in her brother's sacrifice. Hiding her emotions as best she could, she continued to go about her duties in their home, which was permeated more deeply every day by the deathly stillness of the elder woman.

It was, indeed, this pride which buoyed her up without lessening the blow; but in saying to her friend, the teacher of languages, 'I would take liberty from any hand as a hungry man would snatch at a piece of bread. The true progress must begin after. And for that the right men shall be found. They are already amongst us. One comes upon them in their obscurity, unknown, preparing themselves . . . ,' she was thinking not of her brother alone, but of his fellow-student, of whom he had written to her that he was one of those men who lead 'unstained, lofty, and solitary existences,' that fellow-student who was, in fact, Razumov, the man who had betrayed him. Victor Haldin's letters were in her hand as she spoke, and she added, 'His is the only name my brother mentions in all his correspondence with me. Absolutely the only one, and – would you believe it? – the man is here. He arrived recently in Geneva.' (Peter Ivanovitch had told her.)

The situation was fraught with horror, and through stages of bewilderment and, piercing that bewilderment, awakening tenderness for this man whose undemonstrative brusquerie seemed to her innocence the sign of complete integrity, the horror burst upon her. But that lay in the future, and it was, as one may call it, the haunted interregnum which frames, for the book, the story of Nathalie Haldin.

Her one idea was to make the acquaintance of this man who stood above all other men. Surely he could tell them much, surely he could ease their pain! But when the meeting did take place it was like a douche of cold water: Razumov, who had never known that he would find the Haldins in Geneva, was horribly embarrassed to the point of fury and behaved like a mannerless boor. She had gone up to him impulsively, 'Saying with an effort to hide her emotion, "Can't you guess who I am?,"' but he would not even take her hand. 'He even recoiled a step, and Miss Haldin imagined that he was unpleasantly affected,' particularly as he appeared incapable of saying anything beyond a few mumbled words. But she 'excused him, directing her displeasure at herself. She had behaved unworthily, like an emotional French girl. A manifestation of that kind could not be welcomed by a man of stern, self-contained character.'

It was for her so strange a meeting, so utterly different from what she had expected, that none of her excuses, such as the one she made to her friend, 'Mr. Razumov seems to be a man of few words. A reserved man – even when he is strongly moved,' really appeased her aching heart. But she had such faith in her brother's judgment that not for one instant did the shadow of doubt enter her mind: he was a man of rigorously suppressed feelings – that was all. As she confided to her friend, 'He was deeply moved. That I know! In my own agitation I could see it.' And, of course, he *was* 'deeply moved' – but could she have looked beneath the surface . . . !

They met on various other occasions, finally they met every day, but though Razumov was better prepared now, even if fevered by two streams of contrasting emotion, torturing shame and flowering love, and his clumsiness was less, yet, as was inevitable, the fog never lifted. But because she was so trustful, because her directness had its own psychological explanations, she came to this conclusion, as she informed her friend: 'I think that he is observing, studying me, to discover whether I am worthy of his trust . . .' And she went on, after a pause, 'I am convinced . . . . . . that this extraordinary man is meditating some vast plan, some great undertaking; he is possessed by it – he suffers from it – and from being alone in the world.'

The teacher of languages, who was observant and whose wits were sharpened by a sort of jealousy, guessed that there was a stirring in her which, uncomprehended by herself, had taken on a personal tinge, and that Razumov, the man, had begun to attract her: 'The dead brother, the dying mother, the foreign friend, had fallen into a distant background.' Miss Haldin would have been shocked and outraged by such a suggestion, but those words about 'being alone in the world' are apt to be safer indications of the unconscious than a host of denials.

It is true that she was selfless and that, as I said before, she was at heart a revolutionary; but though she may then only have meant that she was ready to help her brother's admired associate in any dangerous undertaking, it seems obvious enough that, unless a personal bond were being forged, his curious behaviour which, however interpreted, was callous – why should future schemes prevent him from telling her of her brother's last hours of freedom? – might finally have disillusioned her. Of course, not being Russian (any more than was the teacher of languages), I may read her all wrong, but in certain aspects of their lives women behave much the same the world over, and my opinion is that her initial enthusiasm for the name of Razumov was assuming a more personal form. She had to excuse him somehow, admittedly, but why should she have jumped at such a far-fetched explanation, and why meet him daily in face of rebuffs?

Indeed, just before the fatal revelation, the teacher of languages, who happened to be present, was conscious, as never previously, of electricity in the air: 'I observed them. There was nothing else to do. My existence seemed so utterly forgotten by those two that I dared not make a movement. But I thought to myself that, of course, they had come together, the sister and the friend of that dead man. The ideas, the hopes, the aspirations, the cause of Freedom, expressed in their common affection for Victor Haldin, the moral victim of autocracy – all this must draw them to each other fatally. Her very ignorance and his loneliness to which he had alluded so strangely must work to that end. And, indeed, I saw that the work was done already . . . . . . I could not mistake the significance of this late visit, for in what he had to say there was nothing urgent. The true cause dawned upon me: he had discovered that he needed her – and she was moved by the same feeling.'

And though in one sense he was totally wrong in his assumptions, in another he was surely right. Razumov had loved her from the first, and she must soon have sensed this love, construing his odd behaviour according to her ardent code; and, in her own manner, she was beginning to respond. (Razumov himself had become aware of the 'possibility of being loved by that admirable girl.') One must remember that, as a young woman, she was both normal and enticing: 'Her voice was deep, almost harsh, and yet caressing in its harshness. She had a dark complexion, with red lips and a full figure. She gave the impression of strong vitality.' The dice were loaded, the scene was set!

After their first unsatisfactory encounter Nathalie Haldin had resolved not yet to tell her mother that Razumov was actually in Geneva and not yet to ask him to call on them. She adhered to this plan until the worsening state of Mrs. Haldin, who had begun to be suspicious of her frequent absences, absences caused by her daily meetings with him, induced her to speak out: 'To remove her suspicions of myself I told her of Mr. Razumov.' Of course, there was excitement at this, also upbraidings for her not having been informed earlier, and in the upshot Miss Haldin, accompanied by the teacher of languages, went off to find Razumov and bring him straight back. And it was during this quest that Razumov, feverishly anxious to tell both women the story about Ziemianitch's suicide, which he himself had just learnt, resolved at last to call. The maid, thinking she was doing the right thing, as she had heard his name mentioned, admitted him at once and announced him to Mrs. Haldin. But it was too late: 'The fifteen minutes with Mrs. Haldin were like the revenge of the unknown: that white face, that weak, distinct voice; that head, turned to him eagerly, then, after a while, bowed again and motionless – in the dim, still light of the room in which his words which he tried to subdue resounded so loudly – had troubled him like some tragic discovery.'

He was, remember, on the verge of his confession to Nathalie, although, when he left his hotel, he had no intention of confessing – just the reverse – and her mother's treatment of him must have seemed like a portent, was perhaps even the deciding factor. She had let him go without a word, for, as we learn later, 'she had not believed him' – a sentence thrilling in its implications. Nathalie assured Razumov, as explaining her strange reception of him, 'You don't know how bad it has come to be. She expects to *see him!*,' and though this might well have accounted for everything – for if in her shattered brain she was sure, to begin with, that he would tell her the joyful news of her son's safety, only to hear a shocking explanation of how his life had been thrown away by the drunkenness of a driver, she may have jumped to the conclusion that Razumov was in league with Nathalie to deceive her. Had not her own daughter kept from her the fact that he was in the town, while seeing him frequently ? What did it mean ? Was vital news being withheld from her ? – and why ? Or perhaps there was something about Razumov himself that spelt for her 'imposter.' People in her mental condition can have their moments of piercing intuition, and possibly her distrust of Razumov was as instinctive as was Nathalie's trust.

In a sense, indeed, the mother's position, tragic as it was, was less terrible than Nathalie's. Both had lost their dearest, who was 'all in all' to them, but while the mother, dreadful as her dreams may have been – for if she now believed her son to be alive, she knew, after the manner of such hallucinations, that something was terribly wrong somewhere – was fading into oblivion and death, the daughter, even through her sorrow, was grasping at a new happiness which was despairingly to elude her.

The revelation was about to fall upon her, but such was her faith in Razumov, such was the rising tide within her, that she could not see the truth, the obvious truth, trying to find utterance in his cryptic words. She was only too conscious that all was not right, but even when she exclaimed, 'You are concealing something from me,' she received no hint of *what* he was concealing: 'Utterly misled by her own enthusiastic interpretation of two lines in the letter of a visionary,' – the letter from her brother mentioning Razumov – 'under the spell of her own dread of lonely days, in their overshadowed world of angry strife, she was unable to see the truth struggling on his lips.' And when, at last, the truth leapt out at her, like a released devil, she was as if felled to the ground. Motionless in the chair into which she had sunk, her first broken words to her friend, himself stricken and almost speechless, 'It is impossible to be more unhappy,' have always seemed to me among the most tragic utterances in literature.

It is witness to the unconquerable fineness of her nature that, after the first blast had spent itself, Nathalie Haldin did not allow this appalling experience to poison her humanity or her idealism. She had, as her friend said, 'completely ceased to think of herself. It was a great victory, a characteristically Russian exploit in self-suppression.' And once again she looked forward, with a fervour that adds music to her sentiments, 'To the day when all discords shall be silenced. Try to imagine its dawn! The tempest of blows and of execrations is over; all is still; the new sun is rising, and the weary men united at last, taking count in their conscience of the ended contest, feeling saddened by their victory, because so many ideas have perished for the triumph of one, so many beliefs have abandoned them without support. They feel alone on the earth and gather close together. Yes, there must be many bitter hours! But at last the anguish of hearts shall be extinguished in love.'

Thus did she speak to her friend, and even if her dream was but a dream, she lived up to its exalted moral. With the death of her mother, which occurred soon after Razumov had had his fruitless interview with her – the teacher of languages was of the opinion that his visit had hastened her end – Nathalie Haldin returned to Russia, 'sharing her compassionate labours between the hideous over-crowded jails and the heartrending misery of bereaved homes.' And this fact, after all she had been through, is her sufficient and shining epitaph.

COUNCILLOR MIKULIN

COUNCILLOR MIKULIN was 'one of those powerful officials who, in a position not obscure, not occult, but simply inconspicuous, exercise a great influence over the methods rather than the conduct of affairs,' and it was natural therefore that it was he who should have had the long official interview with Razumov after the student had denounced Haldin. This is almost his only appearance in *Under Western Eyes*, but he leaves a rather vivid, if amorphous, impression, and as he was responsible for Razumov going to Geneva, he has an importance beyond the obvious. His own personality is kept much in the background, but nevertheless one gets a sort of shadowy, curious view of him which perhaps, at one moment, suggests a clue to his final downfall. When he said to Razumov, 'I understand your liberalism. I have an intellect of that kind myself. Reform for me is mainly a question of method,' he was saying quite sufficient to have aroused the suspicions of a man such as General T—, and many other bureaucrats, even if he continued, 'But the principal of revolt is a physical intoxication, a sort of hysteria which must be kept away from the masses. You agree with this without reserve, don't you? Because, you see, Kirylo Sidorovitch, abstention, reserve, in certain situations, come very near to political crime.' For in an autocracy there must be no hint of reservations, and while the second part of his speech might be regarded as a warning to Razumov, the first part should have been regarded as a warning to himself.

[166]

He was 'a good-natured man and wished no harm to any one,' but this does not imply that, in the execution of his duty, he could not be both crafty and ruthless. To quote Conrad, 'Things and men have always a certain sense, a certain side by which they must be got hold of if one wants to obtain a solid grasp and a perfect command. The power of Councillor Mikulin consisted of his ability to seize upon that sense, that side of the men he used. It did not matter to him what it was – vanity, despair, love, hate, greed, intelligent pride or stupid conceit, it was all one to him as long as the man could be made to serve. The obscure, unrelated young student Razumov, in the moment of great moral loneliness, was allowed to feel that he was an object of interest to a small group of people of high position.' It sounds cynical enough, but in one way or another such methods are universally applied, although with less subtlety and for more obvious reasons.

It must be appreciated that Razumov was not a suspect, save perhaps in the manner in which anybody connected with a political crime in Russia, even the denouncer of the criminal, would be under vague suspicion – his room had already been searched. Mikulin's idea was probably to gain a picture of him as a man who might be potentially useful. But, of course, Razumov, particularly with the knowledge that he was concealing the episode of the drunken Ziemianitch, admission of which would have been highly incriminating, felt himself under suspicion. And that gave a dramatic and revealing turn to the conversation, of which Mikulin took such advantage as was called for.

And his very manner, his trick of leaving sentences unfinished, 'was a deliberate curtailment which somehow made the phrases more impressive.' As for his habit of glancing down his beard, that too, with its air of concealment, must have added to the effect. Maybe, also, the very softness of his voice, the mildness of his words, suggested the ominous pause before the pounce to the student who, in his own heart at any rate, felt himself to be compromised. Razumov's sense of discomfort tended to make him speak heatedly and emphatically out of a sort of nervous bravado, but his furious denunciation of Haldin, 'He was a wretch from my point of view, because to keep alive a false idea is a greater crime than to kill a man. I suppose you will not deny that? I hated him! Visionaries work everlasting evil on earth. Their Utopias inspire in the mass of mediocre minds a disgust of reality and a contempt for the secular logic of human development,' – this denunciation instead of meeting with the immediate, warm approval he must have expected, elicited no response whatsoever: 'The silence and immobility of Councillor Mikulin impressed him. The bearded bureaucrat sat at his post, mysteriously self-possessed like an idol with dim, unreadable eyes.' And doubtless, in a sort of general way which was part of the technique, they were meant to impress him: Councillor Mikulin was well trained in the art of drawing people out.

One cannot help making comparisons between the meetings of Mikulin and Razumov in this book – only one is described, but there were several – and those of Porphiry Petrovitch and Raskolnikov in Dostoevsky's *Crime and Punishment*. They have points of definite resemblance, even down to details, but in essence they are quite different. Talks of this nature, in the circumstances envisaged, were bound to be a strain on the men being questioned, and to that extent reactions were likely to produce rather similar results; but though both the examiners were, in their separate personalities, formidable, in themselves they were quite unalike; and though Razumov and Raskolnikov both had something on their minds they wanted to conceal and both were poor students, in themselves they were utterly different. In brief, the resemblance, though startling, is superficial and probably inevitable, though I admit that it would be very interesting to draw up a complete comparison and discover whether Conrad's purpose was not intended to show how two situations apparently alike can diverge profoundly. I know he had read *Crime and Punishment* – he intensely disliked Dostoevsky – for we once discussed the characters, but I cannot say when he had read it.

Councillor Mikulin was a 'ponderous man' with a 'rugged Socratic forehead,' but physically, despite his beard (or because of it), we scarcely see him. But we learn that he was a 'bachelor with a love of comfort, living alone in an apartment of five rooms luxuriously furnished; and was known to his intimates to be an enlightened patron of the art of female dancing.' In other words, he did himself well in private life and, as it emerges, was a reasonable man in public life, once he was assured that there was nothing significant to discover.

But Razumov, harried by his unfortunate fate and alarmed by his untold secret, could not restrain altogether his temper and his fear, and, as the interview went on and on, suddenly resolved to put all to the test: ' "But, really, I must claim the right to be done once for all with that man. And in order to accomplish this I shall take the liberty . . . " Razumov on his side of the table bowed slightly to the seated bureaucrat. " . . . To retire – simply to retire," he finished with great resolution. He walked to the door, thinking, "Now he must show his hand. He must ring and have me arrested before I am out of the building, or he must let me go. And either way . . . " An unhurried voice said – "Kirylo Sidorovitch." Razumov at the door turned his head. "To retire" he repeated. "Where to?" asked Councillor Mikulin softly.'

There was something that sounded ominous, extremely ominous, in these last two words (they occur on page 99 of Dent's Collected Edition and are not repeated – such is the method of construction – until page 293), but in fact the question 'was not menacing in the least and, indeed, had the ring of innocent enquiry.' And yet there *was* a meaning behind it, and it was this: though Razumov could now take up his former life free of all suspicion, he would, sooner or later, return to take up another life. Mikulin was very sure of this, and his parting words, 'We live in difficult times, in times of monstrous chimeras and evil dreams and criminal follies. We shall certainly meet once more. It may be some little time, though, before we do. Till then may Heaven send you fruitful reflections!' have a kind of prophetic ring which could not be ignored. Indeed, they *did* meet again, when Mikulin, who had meanwhile been appointed to the important post of directing the 'general police supervision of Europe,' remembered 'that uncommon young man on whom he had a hold already, with his peculiar temperament, his unsettled mind and shaken conscience, struggling in the toils of a false position,' and induced him to go to Geneva, where it was known that a 'very serious plot was being matured,' as a Government spy.

What we gather personally of Mikulin during his conversation with Razumov is practically nothing, for even his frankness was not without its ulterior motive; but we do seem to get a strange, true glimpse of him when, a few years later, he fell into disgrace: 'In the stir of vaguely seen monstrosities, in that momentary, mysterious disturbance of muddy waters, Councillor Mikulin went under, dignified, with only a calm, emphatic protest of his innocence – nothing more. No disclosures damaging to a harassed autocracy, complete fidelity to the secrets of that miserable *arcana imperii* deposited in a patriotic breast, a display of bureaucratic stoicism in a Russian official's ineradicable, almost sublime contempt for truth; stoicism of silence understood only by the very few of the initiated, and not without a certain cynical grandeur of self-sacrifice on the part of the sybarite. For the terribly heavy sentence turned Councillor Mikulin civilly into a corpse, and actually into something very much like a common convict.' Had that liberal streak in him, which does not sound like a pose, led to rashness or was he the victim of some fantastically obscure political complication only the official Russian mind could invent or unravel? Who can say? All we know definitely is that this enigmatic man was faithful to his code.

And perhaps we were never meant to know any more, perhaps Councillor Mikulin was a symbol as well as a personality, a victim of the incohate, elemental forces, plunging ahead like a somnambulist and, in their inner workings, complex without being efficient. He was a cog in a machine, useful or broken as the machine functioned smoothly or developed defects, but anyhow, for all his ability, no more than an interpreter of a system which, in itself, was moving in a direction no one could foretell, but suggestive somehow of that 'monstrous blank page awaiting the record of an inconceivable history,' to which Razumov had compared the snow-bound winter night of Russia.

Conrad was a realist who disapproved altogether of the type of symbolism represented by such a work as Herman Melville's *Moby Dick*, a book which he detested, and yet surely there is in some of his own fiction a sort of inevitable realistic symbolism.

For example, just as Captain MacWhirr of *Typhoon* suggests, for all his reality, something symbolic of man's mastery over the powers of nature, and Kurtz of *Heart of Darkness* suggests, for all his reality, something symbolic of the corrupting forces of the wilderness, so does Mikulin, real enough in himself, seem to symbolise a Government attitude so formless and barren as to grasp at shadows rather than face problems.

PETER IVANOVITCH

THE DARKENED GLASSES always worn by Peter Ivanovitch, making it impossible to get a clear view of his expression, emphasise the difficulty of gaining an accurate conception of the man himself. That he had undergone terrible perils and hardships in Siberia is true, and Conrad devotes pages to a vivid and harrowing account of them; but it is also true that he had written a highly successful book describing his adventures and that, frightful as they were and bravely as he had borne them, they had really been the making of his career, which was that of an instigator and planner of revolutionary activities in Russia from the safe refuge of Switzerland or the south of France.

He had, says the teacher of languages, 'one of those bearded Russian faces without shape, a mere appearance of flesh and hair with not a single feature having any sort of character,' and that is descriptive of him in more ways than one. No doubt he was genuine enough in his revolutionary philosophy, but though his conversation was often of an exalted nature he was, in private life, liable to be extremely petty and self-centred, and Razumov got the idea that his apparent devotion for the rich Madame de S——, an 'ancient, painted mummy,' was decidedly financial.

The person who really gave Peter Ivanovitch away as a human being was his secretary (Madame de S——'s companion), Tekla, a woman so simple, guileless and straightforward that, malicious as her words often sound, they were probably intended rather

as statements of fact than utterances of a personal grievance. As
she admitted to Miss Haldin, 'Peter Ivanovitch is the greatest
genius of the century perhaps, but he is the most inconsiderate
man living,' and, again, 'After taking down Peter Ivanovitch
from dictation for two years, it is difficult for me to be anything.
First of all, you have to sit perfectly motionless. The slightest
movements you make puts to flight the ideas of Peter Ivanovitch. You hardly dare to breathe. And as to coughing – God
forbid. Peter Ivanovitch changed the position of the table to the
wall because at first I could not help raising my eyes to look out
of the window, while waiting for him to go on with his dictation. That was not allowed. He said I stared so stupidly. I was
likewise not permitted to look at him over my shoulder. In-
stantly Peter Ivanovitch stamped his foot, and would roar,
"Look down at the paper!" It seems my expression, my face,
put him off. Well, I know that I am not beautiful, and that my
expression is not hopeful either. He said that my air of unintelli-
gent expectation irritated him.'

Of course, even great men have their weaknesses and obviously Tekla got on his nerves, but it seems a little odd that so
outstanding a feminist, who was constantly praising the noble
souls of women, should have behaved so harshly to the poor
feminine creature who was helping him. Even assuming, which
is not likely, that Tekla exaggerated, Miss Haldin's own obser-
vations bore her out. When, after waiting some time to meet
the genius, she told him on his arrival that she was sorry she
would have to leave now as she was anxious to get back to her
mother, he responded, ' "The time seemed long, eh? I am afraid
our worthy friend here" (Peter Ivanovitch suddenly jerked his
head sideways towards his right shoulder and jerked it up again)
– "our worthy friend here has not the art of shortening the

[174]

moments of waiting. No, distinctly she has not the art; and in that respect good intentions alone count for nothing." ' It is not astonishing that 'Miss Haldin was extremely indignant on behalf of the lady companion.'

Like many other people, Peter Ivanovitch loved power, but whether that was a personal instinct or designed to help the cause is not made plain: perhaps there was something of both in this love. Tekla once said to Razumov, when he had expressed surprise at the revolutionist's efforts to keep in touch with Miss Haldin, 'Don't you understand that Peter Ivanovitch must direct, inspire, influence? It is the breath of his life. There can never be too many disciples. He can't bear thinking of any one escaping him. And a woman, too! There is nothing to be done without woman, he says.' And this evidently included secretarial work, though not the comfort or susceptibilities of the secretary. Had he flourished in a later epoch, Peter Ivanovitch, one feels, might almost have become a fashionable craze, ladies flocking to listen to his thunderbolts, larded with compliments about their sex, in the intervals of tea being handed round. How he would have expanded in such an environment!

However, all these are but sidelights on his personality, witnesses to the well-known fact that a great figure may also be a bit of a tyrant and a bit of a snob, and do not necessarily indicate that he was merely a hollow sham. He must surely have been more than that, or otherwise how could he have maintained his prestige in revolutionary circles which, one imagines, are quick to criticise and condemn? Even Sophia Antonovna, who was not too easily imposed upon, appeared to be quite blind to his defects, as caustically pointed out to her by Razumov, for she announced in the very last words of the novel, 'Peter Ivanovitch is an inspired man.'

And perhaps he was, but in what way? Assuredly he had a commanding background and probably he was skilled in organisation, but, quite apart from any faults in his character, he seems to have been rather dull except when he was holding forth, when he seems to have been rather tactless. At any rate, this is the impression one gathers, though it may be that his fame was derived from his books rather than from his talk. Or perhaps his was one of those reputations which, for some reason or other, is taken for granted even by the sceptical. One simply does not know, but Conrad's contemptuous reference to him – he said in his Author's Note to *Under Western Eyes*, 'Peter Ivanovitch and Madame de S— are fair game. They are the apes of a sinister jungle and are treated as their grimaces deserve' – does not make it easier to comprehend why he should have been able to hold his position in the 'jungle' with such unquestioned authority, unless Conrad meant to imply that the revolutionists, as a body, were just a flock of silly sheep ready to follow any leader.

We first meet Peter Ivanovitch when he calls upon the Haldins to condole with them over the death of the son and brother, but Miss Haldin, who received him for them both, was not favourably impressed by what he said, although there was something rather monumental in the appearance he presented to her: 'He towered before her, enormous, deferential, cropped as close as a convict; and his big pinkish poll evoked for me' – the teacher of languages is the observer – 'the vision of a wild head with matted locks peering through parted bushes, glimpses of naked, tawny limbs slinking behind the masses of sodden foliage under a cloud of flies and mosquitoes. It was an involuntary tribute to the vigour of his writing. Nobody could doubt that he had wandered in Siberian forests, naked and girt with a chain.

[176]

The black broadcloth coat invested his person with a character of austere decency – something recalling a missionary.' But here, once more, the total effect is rather confused.

But when Peter Ivanovitch began to speak of his Egeria, that 'old harridan' Madame de S—, his rhapsodic words ring so false that they set one's teeth on edge: 'She is a perpetual manifestation of a noble and peerless spirit . . . . . . Her charm – no, I shall not speak of her charm. But, of course, everybody who approaches her falls under the spell . . . Contradictions vanish, troubles fall away from one.' Leading out of this eulogy, he continued, 'Unless I am mistaken – but I never make a mistake in spiritual matters – you are troubled in your soul, Natalia Victorovna.' Miss Haldin's friend had the notion, on this, that he 'could be as impudent as he chose;' and as for Miss Haldin, who had listened to him for more than an hour, with only one brief display of impatience when he had been particularly maladroit, her remark, on being asked for some particulars – 'He is a revolutionary feminist, a great writer, if you like' – did not strike the note of enthusiasm.

We are left very much where we were before, and the secret of his dominance still eludes us. With Razumov he tried to be friendly, for not only was he the man of the hour but he hoped to inveigle him into a plot he was hatching, and he even attempted heavy flattery: 'You are close, very close. This taciturnity, this severe brow, this something inflexible and secret in you, inspires hopes and a little wonder as to what you may mean. There is something of a Brutus . . . ' How fatuous and forced it sounds, and we get a sort of satisfaction from the reply, ' "Pray spare me those classical allusions!" burst out Razumov nervously. "What comes Junius Brutus to do here? It is ridiculous!" '

It *was* ridiculous, and so, one cannot help thinking, was the great man himself. Is he, perhaps, too much of a caricature and, by being that, does he cease to be psychologically coherent? Conrad usually kept a pretty tight rein on his figures, but in this case satire and realism are so mixed that we hardly know what is intended. For every now and then, when our minds are made up in one direction, Peter Ivanovitch says or does something which gives us a fresh slant in another direction. For example, when we learn near the end that, Madame de S— having died without making a will, her devoted friend and admirer had 'united himself to a peasant girl' and had seemingly – though this is not altogether clear – returned to Russia, it is as if the buffoon has changed into a man. Or was it but another pose to fit the altered conditions?

SOPHIA ANTONOVNA

ALTHOUGH Sophia Antonovna is slightly boring with her constant, contemptuous, but not ill-natured, remarks – many instances could be quoted – about the density of men, a middle-class habit one might suppose such a convinced revolutionist to have despised, yet it is a relief to write of her after writing of Peter Ivanovitch, for, at any rate, she was direct and easy in her speech, tireless in her selfless activities, and quite without ego-tism. She appears to have been a sort of underground courier and was almost perpetually on the move.

Razumov had met her first in Zürich, where he had broken his journey on the way from Dresden to Geneva, and when she turned up in the latter town, 'she was wearing the very same costume in which he had seen her first. A blouse of crimson silk made her noticeable at a distance. With that she wore a short brown skirt and a leather belt. Her complexion was the colour of coffee and milk, but very clear; her eyes black and glittering, her figure erect. A lot of thick hair, nearly white, was done up loosely under a dusty Tyrolese hat of dark cloth, which seemed to have lost some of its trimmings.' Not an unattractive woman for her age, if a bit dowdy, and the more so as her expression was 'grave, intent; so grave that Razumov, after approaching her close, felt obliged to smile. She greeted him with a manly hand-grasp.'

From the moment of their first meeting, Razumov had been rather favourably impressed by her personally, although he judged her to be a 'distinct danger in his path. "Judged" is not perhaps the right word. It was more of a feeling, the summing up of slight impressions aided by the discovery that he could not despise her as he despised all the others.' That she should have perceived at once that 'what's the matter with you is that you don't like us' was, in itself, of small account, though it was no doubt as well to be forewarned; but as good luck would have it, he need not have given it a second thought, as the few details she had learnt from correspondents in St. Petersburg of events subsequent to the bomb-throwing all helped either to build up his reputation as a man of iron nerve, or to abolish completely the vague suspicion with which some of the revolutionists had regarded him. For just after the assassination he had been seen in the lecture-room calmly making notes, and it was now proved that it was the drunkenness of Ziemianitch, who had, as we know, hanged himself out of remorse, which had foiled Haldin's plan for escape.

Everything was going even better than Razumov could have hoped, but his bantering tone, which, in his 'envenomed reck-lessness,' he could not control, caused Sophia Antonovna to say tartly, 'Leave off railing . . . . . Remember, Razumov, that women, children, and revolutionists hate irony, which is the negation of all saving instincts, of all faith, of all devotion, of all action.' She was a fairly intelligent woman, but she wore the blinkers of a preconceived attitude, blinkers never removed, and must thus have missed many of the nuances which, as a profes-sional revolutionist, should surely have given her various useful hints. It would seem to a reader, indeed, that had she not jumped too readily to certain conclusions, which a more probing intel-lect would have questioned, matters would not perhaps have turned out so conveniently for Razumov. She felt convinced, for instance, that it was 'some scoundrelly detective' who had beaten Ziemianitch, but this was merely an unsubstantiated theory. In fact, all her talk on the subject, all her apparently reasonable assumptions, were based on a false premise. This, of course, is the commonest of errors; but for a woman such as Sophia Antonovna, who brushed subtleties aside as unworthy of so vital and serious a cause, the complexities of human reactions and the infinite gradations of emotional experience were things to be consciously ignored. But even she, who had simplified everything, should have known better.

The long conversation she had with Razumov, covering between forty and fifty pages, is practically all we see of Sophia Antonovna, but despite her destructive approach to society and her calm assumption of ultimate truth, she creates a good impression. At any rate, she was a real person, as dedicated as any nun – when Razumov questions her on her belief that 'everything is bound to come right in the end,' and asks, 'You think so?,' her reply, 'I don't think, young man, I just simply believe it,' would have pleased the most mystic of Christian apologists. And there was no posing, no exaggeration in her language. She behaved as she preached, and was evidently uttering what, to her, was a truism when she said to Razumov, 'You have begun well, but you just wait till you have trodden every particle of yourself under your feet in your comings and goings. For that is what it comes to. You've got to trample down every particle of your own feelings.'

In truth, the more one listens to her, the more she reminds one of a mediaeval saint who, through some kink of reasoning or, if you like, some independence of mind, has found herself in the wrong camp. For example, 'You have either to rot or to burn. And there is not one of us, painted or unpainted, who would not rather burn than rot.' Or, 'Life, Razumov, not to be vile must be a revolt – a pitiless protest – all the time.' These may not be the words a religious devotee would employ, but, in their fiery sincerity, their sentiments could readily be translated into moral truths by an ardent pietistic reformer.

Razumov, of course, detested her sentiments, particularly when she spoke of the 'uncompromising sense of necessity and justice which armed your and Haldin's hands to strike down that fanatical brute,' his own feelings being, 'As if anything could be changed! In this world of men nothing can be changed – neither happiness nor misery. They can only be displaced at the cost of corrupted consciences and broken lives – a futile game for arrogant philosophers and sanguinary triflers.' But all the same he did not scorn 'the respected, trusted, and influential Sophia Antonovna, whose word had such a weight in the "active" section of the party.' He had been relieved, naturally, to learn that she proposed to return to Zürich on the following day, for self-protection was still strong within him, and it also gave him a 'feeling of triumphant pleasure to deceive her out of her own mouth;' but she did not exasperate him, as did the other revolutionaries, and she was the only one with whom he would have held a conversation of such length. Even her talk of 'destructive revolution,' however distasteful, could be shrugged off, for had she not given up everything worth having in order to justify her bigotry?

And though she had urged upon Razumov the necessity to 'trample down every particle of your own feelings,' it is clear that when she spoke of Yakovlitch, a revolutionary just returned from America where he had been for fifteen years, there was a kind of nostalgic softness in her memories of long ago, however quickly repressed. Equally, though she explained, later, her occasional visits to the dying Razumov in that remote Russian village as due to his intelligence and ideas, it is evident that she was not without pity, however disguised, for that unhappy man. Sophia Antonovna was, indeed, one of those women born to give out more than she received, completely lacking in self-pity on the one hand or a desire to shine on the other. And such a woman's character must arouse some respect and perhaps even some envy.

5

CHANCE

1913

THE GOVERNESS

FLORA DE BARRAL'S governess, that sinister woman whose treatment of her charge in her hour of need leaves its indelible stain, poisoning her youth and deeply affecting her destiny, makes but a brief actual appearance in *Chance*; and yet, such was Conrad's power of evocation, she rises before us with a kind of shuddering intensity. No name is given to her, she emerges, as it were, out of the darkness and vanishes into the darkness; but this woman of forty, with her manner of severe propriety, her air of 'cold distinguished exclusiveness' and, underneath it all, the 'soul of a remorseless brigand,' is as vitally portrayed as almost any figure in the whole of Conrad's gallery.

'She was,' says Marlow, the narrator who plays his part in so many of Conrad's books, 'abominable, but she was not common.' Indeed, she was not; she was very uncommon – far-sighted, resolute, self-contained and implacable. Had she been an ordinary adventuress she might have set her cap at de Barral, the fabulously rich widower, but she had always treated him 'with an assured, distant politeness,' thus maintaining her prestige, while secretly despising and detesting both father and daughter. Moreover, avid and hungry, she had a passionate nature which she had had to suppress as essential to her pose of superior governess, and now that she had seen 'her youth vanish, her freshness disappear, her hopes die, and ...... felt her flaming middle-age slipping away from her,' she had formed, perhaps as a sort of desperate last throw, an infatuation for a worthless young blackguard, who passed as her nephew and was just as unscrupulous and heartless as herself.

We know as little about Charley as we know about her – his beginnings, his surname, or where they had met – but one can imagine the swift glance of recognition, the voiceless message passing between them. Like calls to like, and they were both morally lawless and rotten at the core. Charley, in his male self-sufficiency, was simpler, infinitely simpler, than the governess, but in his own way he was just as vile; and she, being free of illusions and 'terribly practical,' knew that she could only hold him, so much younger than herself (he was twenty-three), so utterly devoid of unselfishness and gratitude, so completely egocentric and grasping, by dangling before his eyes an irresistible bait. And this was no less than to marry him off to Flora de Barral.

It sounds fantastic, and it was fantastic. But then, as Marlow remarks, to be without illusions does not mean to be reasonable. Again, to quote his words, 'the subterfuges of a menaced passion are not to be fathomed,' and it might have worked. Yes, it might have worked. He was the only young man whom Flora, shut up with her governess in that large Brighton house, her mother dead and her father in London, had ever met, and because he was good-looking in a raffish style and had cultivated a ready charm, she was greatly attached to him. They used to go out riding together like gay adventurers and she had come to look forward to the visits of her governess's 'nephew' with immense pleasure. Not yet quite sixteen, she was untouched by love, but things ripen and ripen, and one day the plot might have succeeded. But what of the governess in that case? Marlow suggests that, already aware how age was telling against her, she only looked a few years ahead; but might she not have envisaged other possibilities?

And then suddenly, out of the blue, the first hint of de Barral's financial collapse! Her security gone, her schemes frustrated, the very basis of everything overthrown, the defeated woman had to act immediately, for there were still a few matters to attend to before she disappeared. And the chief of these was to vent her fury on Flora. For apart from her envenomed antipathy and apart from the fact that it was through the girl's father that she had been ruined monetarily and emotionally, Flora, in her defencelessness, personified for her 'all the accumulated dislike for all her pupils, her scorn of all her employers . . . . . . the accumulated resentment, the infinite hatred of all those unrelieved years.' The time had come to settle the score!

Enjoying his unpaid-for comforts, Charley wanted to linger on a few days – what was the urgent hurry? – but not so the governess: 'From the very first, somehow, she had accepted the fatal news as true. All her life she had never believed in her luck, with that pessimism of the passionate who at bottom feel themselves to be the outcasts of a morally restrained universe.' And anyhow, unspoken, there was the determination that there was to be 'no more of that boy and girl philandering since the object of it was gone.'

Charley, who had a speck, if not of decency, of masculine embarrassment, would have left the looted house without attempting to see Flora again, especially as he was now in possession of the money de Barral had deposited in the name of the governess at a local bank; but that did not suit the woman's plan, perhaps because she was out to destroy, amongst other things, Flora's faith in her one male friend and take from her even the consolation of her memories. He was persuaded to accompany her to the drawing-room, where the girl, exhilarated by her painting lesson from the genial old teacher who had just left, was sitting relaxed and carefree. All at once the door opened and 'Charley walked in with his eyes fixed on the back of the governess . . . . . . The girl was astounded and alarmed by the altogether unknown expression in the woman's face . . . . . . There was something like an emanation of evil from her eyes and from the face of the other, who, exactly behind her and overtopping her by half a head, kept his eyelids lowered in a sinister fashion.' It is the scene that follows, a monstrous revelation of concealed cruelty and wickedness, and the shock it engenders, which build, as one might say, the very background of *Chance*.

Even if we knew much more about the governess than we do, it would probably be impossible and, if possible, largely unprofitable to attempt any coherent analysis of her personality. She revolves in an obscure anarchic world in which the accepted moral values are ignored, although, in the irony of things, it was on their rigid outward observance that her career had been based. Entirely rapacious by instinct, her inherent contempt for society and its taboos encased her like an impervious shell within which the fierce beat of her desires went on uncontrolled. But all the same, depraved as she was, she was tragic in her downfall. Behind her facade of 'never-failing correctness,' developed to perfection by the concentrated force of her will, she had lived like a ravening wolf in a cage. Her longing for a vicious freedom, for the colour of an existence without even the hint of inhibitions, had been stifled year after year – and all to no avail! No doubt she had had her chances, spurned by her as not good enough; no doubt also men had been frightened off by that something imponderably dangerous about her; but now, when only too conscious of time she had at last achieved a precarious equilibrium, the blow had fallen. All that was left to her was the cold, hopeless isolation of her despair.

Of course, it is Conrad's searching and creative insight and his mastery of atmosphere which add the final touch of macabre verisimilitude to the governess and her surroundings, compelling us to watch breathlessly, as the Fynes watched, the unfolding of this gloomy drama. But over and above, she represents that feeling of the treachery of life, of deadly forces lying in wait for us when least expected, that seems to have haunted Conrad's mind, for into several of his novels there enter, as a miasma might enter, malignant, crafty, disruptive figures to undermine every bulwark of security and warn us against complacent ease even in the midst of apparent safety.

THE FYNES

IF I BRACKET the names of Fyne and his wife under one head-
ing, it is partly because they are, as a team, inextricably mixed up
with the fate of Flora de Barral, and partly because they appear,
in all their dissimilarity, to be so complementary that we can
hardly imagine one without the other. When we are shown
them at the window of their hotel, watching the de Barral house,
Fyne standing beside his seated wife 'as in those old-fashioned
photographs of married couples where you see a husband with
his hand on the back of his wife's chair,' the picture they make
might be a symbol of their inseparability.

Of course, this is an exaggeration, for Conrad draws them
convincingly, very convincingly, both as individuals and as man
and woman; but nevertheless, in a way eluding definition, they
do give one the impression of forming an entity. Perhaps it is
bound up with their general approach to life, so conscientious,
serious-minded and humourless; but there is something more
subtle in it than that, some aura, which Conrad conveys with
marvellous skill.

In themselves the Fynes were an ordinary middle-class couple,
he an ardent practical pedestrian, she an ardent theoretical
feminist, leading the conventional existence of their sort, and
it is curious to note how their involvement with the affairs of
Flora de Barral, so alien to anything that had happened to them
before, brings out unexpected aspects of their characters. It even
produced a disagreement between them – an unheard of thing!

– and although the illusion of their basic oneness was only cracked, it does seem to let in a shaft of revealing light.

The Fynes were humane people and they did their best for the unfortunate Flora in very difficult circumstances. But because Mrs. Fyne's temperament was cold even in its compassion and unimaginative even in its justice – Fyne in all such matters automatically following her lead to begin with – their help, extended over years, did not heal the injury the girl had suffered, and no true bond was established. Mrs. Fyne lived by a set of rules which, however carefully formulated, were really an expression of her personality, and though she found the problem of Flora disturbing and distasteful, the relationship, such as it was, might have continued indefinitely, had not something happened to arouse personal reactions. And this was the arrival of her brother, Captain Roderick Anthony, on the scene. It was then that the Fynes, floundering out of their depth, began to exhibit unknown traits. Her chilly kindness turned to active resentment, and his echoing acquiescence discovered a sympathy for the girl which placed him in unbelievable opposition.

Fyne was a Civil Servant, and though Conrad can have had very little experience of this class he draws him with a sureness of touch only to be ascribed to a deeply intuitive perception which, while disentangling the individual from the type, gives to the type its due significance. An established institution, such as the Civil Service, throws a certain air of sameness over its higher executives, stamping them, as any recognised profession stamps a body of men, with the mark of its traditions. But this veneer is superficial, save in the densely self-satisfied, and although the instant we learn that Fyne belonged to the Civil Service, we see 'Civil Service' written all over him, the quality of Fyne himself is just as apparent. He was a precise, solemn man – in fact, as

Marlow quaintly remarks, his solemnity 'extended to the very eating of bread and butter;' but his tastes, which consisted of chess and walking, were straightforward, simple and exactly what might have been expected.

In public life he was doubtless reliable, painstaking and rather stubborn, one of those men who do their work competently and, without thrusting themselves forward unduly, indefatigably. In private life he allowed himself to be managed by his wife, and if, at the correct seasons, he was wrapped up in his hobbies, he must have been a devoted husband and father, probably devoid of social or material ambitions. In a word, he was just like thousands of prosaically happy married men. But there was another Fyne, the Fyne who had eloped with the daughter of the tyrannical poet, Carleon Anthony, the Fyne who, when called upon to act in a crisis, as in the rescue of the half-demented Flora de Barral, displayed immediate efficiency: 'He was at the door before she reached it in her blind course. She did not recognise him; perhaps she did not see him. He caught her by the arm as she ran past and, very sensibly, without trying to check her, simply darted in with her and up the stairs, causing no end of consternation amongst the people in his way. They scattered. What might have been their thoughts at the spectacle of a middle-aged man abducting headlong into the upper regions of a respectable hotel a terrified young girl obviously under age, I don't know. And Fyne (he told me so) did not care for what people might think. All he wanted was to reach his wife before the girl collapsed.'

Again, there was a sensitive streak in Fyne which, under pressures stirring him out of his regular habits and frame of mind, emerged from beneath his Civil Service mantle of discretion and understatement to confound his wife. There had always been signs of this sensitiveness even in his negative attitude, but it needed Mrs. Fyne's firm resolve to stop Flora marrying Captain Anthony that really brought it into the open in defence of one who had endured such undeserved calamities. Did he not say to Marlow that 'it would take a lot to persuade him to "push under the head of a poor devil of a girl quite sufficiently plucky." ' And when, on Marlow's advice, he at last consented to go to London to see Anthony on his wife's behalf, he did so in a spirit of obvious ill-nature, not far short of rebellion, extremely foreign to his retiring disposition.

And this ill-nature, turning into indignation after his meeting with his brother-in-law, whose manner seemed to the unperceptive Fyne deplorably flippant, revealed still another facet of his character. It is difficult to imagine active anger in the dominated little Fyne, but then, as Marlow observes, his 'solemnity had got damaged somehow . . . . . . there were holes in it through which I could see a new, an unknown Fyne.'

In everybody, of course, there are unsuspected possibilities, but for a man like Fyne, who was not introspective, cause and effect are little understood, and their disintegrating influence, not being rationalised, would naturally, in such an untoward case, lead to chaotic reactions. Had he not had a disagreement with his wife – which, one may be sure, was carried on in the quietest manner, she calmly adamant, he responding intermittently by low growls of excuse or dissent – and thus felt himself uprooted, he would never have approached his unwelcome task in a spirit ready to take offence and, indeed, in so touchy a mood that he was bound, not only to fail, but to widen the breach. But he was behaving untrue to type because, in the upset of his balance, he had unconsciously adopted a truculent pose as a self-protective mechanism.

In getting out of his stride Fyne was gaining experience, but losing continuity. And in the long run, with a character such as his, it is continuity which gives cohesion and cohesion which gives meaning. His mind had the orderliness of a man in a smooth and accustomed rut, and he was so set in his ways that his lapse would obviously only be temporary: the symbiosis between Fyne and his wife would soon function again to their mutual advantage, and once more he would fill his niche, the one niche he could fill, with perfect satisfaction.

For the time being, however, he had lost his balance; but Mrs. Fyne, who had also lost her balance, was dogmatic by nature and quite unaware of any mental conflict. For all her aggresive feminism, she was excessively feminine, just as Fyne, for all his subservience to her theories, was excessively masculine. The only way to get on with Mrs. Fyne, to come within the orbit of her understanding, was to agree with her. But in Flora de Barral, whom she had befriended for years without finding in her a co-operative pupil, she had met some one who upset her cherished conviction that women are always in the right. Mrs. Fyne's philosophy was uncomplicated by light or shade. As Marlow puts it: 'Shortly, and so far as my bewilderment allowed me to grasp its naive atrociousness, it was something like this: that no consideration, no delicacy, no tenderness, no scruples should stand in the way of a woman (who by the mere fact of her sex was the predestined victim of conditions created by men's selfish passions, their vices and their abominable tyranny) from taking the shortest cut towards securing for herself the easiest possible existence.'

This, no doubt, is too ruthless an interpretation of Mrs. Fyne's principles (which, however, were quite ruthless enough), or otherwise her ideal of womanly behaviour would have been

Flora's unscrupulous governess. But her actual conduct was constantly being modified by her disposition, for, as Marlow says, her 'audacity was in her thoughts,' and anyhow she was a human being and, before all, a woman. She repudiated the governess without question because she detested her personally; she repudiated Flora without question because she felt she must protect her brother. The governess, in her sheer evil, was probably the exception that proves the rule; but when Flora, behaving, to the provoked astonishment of Mrs. Fyne, as an independent woman and not as a helpless waif, announced that, though she did not love Captain Anthony, she intended to marry him for reasons of her own, then Mrs. Fyne's precepts went by the board. And so, without perceiving that she was being actuated by the very reverse of her beliefs, she determined to prevent the match – although, incidentally, she did not care in the least for her brother.

What finally turned her against Flora was the letter which the girl wrote to her after surreptitiously leaving the Fyne's house for ever. At the end of the book we learn from Flora's own lips about this letter, and her words may be quoted here, always bearing in mind that, unable to help her father, now on the eve of being released from prison, by her own efforts and holding passionately to his innocence, she was ready to jump at any opportunity in face of his dependence on her and the injustice of the world. She was like a blind, terrified creature not knowing where to turn and frantically sniffing the air. 'I was feeling reckless,' she said, 'and I wrote recklessly. I knew she would disapprove and I wrote foolishly. It was the echo of her own stupid talk. I said that I did not love her brother and that I had no scruples whatever in marrying him.'

Mrs. Fyne never showed this letter even to her husband, a fact emphasised on several occasions, but she gave him a version of it which caused him to remark to Marlow, 'My wife has her own ideas, but this is an outrageous misapprehension of her views' – even if shortly afterwards, in a bewildered effort to be equitable, he added, with reference to Flora, 'For myself I don't blame her. No! by heavens I don't blame her.' But is it not more probable that Flora's words, far from being a misapprehension of Mrs. Fyne's views, reduced them to absurdity by giving only too exact a rendering of her theories in order to explain her own conduct? There is a kind of implied, contemptuous ridicule that even Mrs. Fyne, armoured though she was, would have shrunk from repeating; and this, one may reasonably suppose, was why she would not allow the actual words to be seen. How often it happens that the tone in which things are said is of more significance than the words, as if it coloured them specially for the recipient, and Flora, desperate in her helplessness, must have wounded Mrs. Fyne to the quick by her apparent ingratitude and mockery. And thus, smarting, in her literal-mindedness, from what the girl had written, and recalling all she had done for her, Mrs. Fyne's natural fairness would be overwhelmed by a wave of indignation.

But Marlow was of the opinion that there might have been a more sinuous reason for Mrs. Fyne's drastic attitude, which was that, by doing what she did, she was making certain that they would never be bothered again by this uncomfortable and un-wanted pair: 'She did not hope to stop anything. She had too much sense for that . . . . . . She wanted the protest to be made emphatically, with Fyne's fullest concurrence, in order to make all intercourse for the future impossible.' Marlow admitted that this might have been an unconscious reason, and I am convinced that this is the only way in which such a reason could possibly

[198]

be accepted even as a supposition. For Mrs. Fyne was neither subtle nor calculating. On the contrary, she was direct and – within the bounds of her code, which, in its turn, affected her judgment – charitable. Her manner was always collected, her thoughts frequently disapproving, but her conduct, when in command of herself, invariably just. One must not underrate Mrs. Fyne's character, which though narrow, boring and dogmatic, was upright. More than most of us she was all of a piece, and when Conrad describes her waiting at the door of her bedroom for the rescued Flora 'with her quite unmoved physiognomy and her readiness to confront any sort of responsibility,' he is giving us a portrait of the whole woman. She was what she appeared to be, disciplined through and through.

It is true that she soon came to the conclusion that the collapsed Flora was 'too emotional – much too emotional to be ever really sound,' but this did not prevent her from comforting the girl to the best of her capacity. As Marlow comments, her 'patient immobility by the bedside of that brutally murdered childhood did infinite honour to her humanity. That vigil must have been the more trying because I could see very well that at no time did she think the victim particularly charming or sympathetic. It was a manifestation of pure compassion, of compassion in itself, so to speak, not many women would have been capable of displaying with that unflinching steadiness.'

But the really admirable thing was the persistence of her kindness, her ceaseless hospitality, to this girl with her anti-pathetic personality and the shadow of her convict father hanging over her. It was often inconvenient to have her in the house, particularly as she was not popular even with the children, but Mrs. Fyne did not allow this to make any difference. Flora, who had always been a problem, had now become an insoluble problem, and yet Mrs. Fyne, fortified no more by her sense of duty than by her inherent, if undemonstrative, charity, would never, in the usual run of things, have got rid of her. 'What else could we do?' she exclaimed to Marlow, who adds, 'that little cry of distress, quite genuine in its inexpressiveness, altered my feeling towards Mrs. Fyne. It would have been so easy to have done nothing and to have thought no more about it.'

Indeed, we must give Mrs. Fyne her due, and if she did lose her balance and behave out of character, let us remember that she had had a horrible jolt and, according to her way of thinking, a disgraceful revelation. And this may excuse her for writing to her brother, 'for years I tried to make a friend of that girl, but I warn you once more that she has the nature of a heartless adventuress.' Poor Mrs. Fyne, poor Flora!

We can, as I observed earlier, safely leave the Fynes to their mutual recovery, in which, we may assume, Flora's name was banned for ever; for unlike the Anthonys, who also experienced a marital difference which brought them to the edge of disaster, they were neither tortured by doubt nor cast in a heroic mould.

FLORA

WERE IT NOT FOR the final chapter of *Chance* in which, at last, we see Flora free of worry and in her real light, it would be impossible to disentangle her character, so distorted was it by the shock she had suffered in her youth and so weighed down by endless misfortunes. Indeed, those closing sentences were called for to let us perceive the inner quality of her personality. 'She was now,' says Marlow, 'her true self, she was like a fine tranquil afternoon,' going on from that description to present her to us in the delicate shades of her generous, loyal and sensitive nature.

And yet, in retrospect, and allowing for the inevitable development from youth to maturity, much that emerges in the end can be glimpsed throughout her whole story. From the beginning one feels her fundamental simplicity and directness which, if over-ingenuous on occasion, was always quite natural. For she had that brand of instinctive integrity which does not even envisage acting a part as a means to momentary success or as a method of normal appeasement.

In brief, she was the very type of girl, as completely unaware of evil as of any of the other positive forces of life, on whom the sudden revelation of it would fall with the most frightful effect. We must remember that for years her governess had been to Flora a mentor and a guide, the moulder of her whole existence, and that between them there was 'an intimacy of relation as great as it can possibly be without the final closeness of affection;'

and that thus, when without any warning at all everything was shattered in a scene of incredible ferocity, a scene of revenge both personal and cosmic, the girl was hopelessly overwhelmed. When the governess, accompanied by Charley, entered the room and Flora, in a flash of illumination, saw that the masks had been dropped and her safe world hideously undermined, the effect was so total that it 'reached, stirred, set free that faculty of unreasoning explosive terror lying locked at the bottom of all human hearts . . . . . . With suddenly enlarged pupils and a movement as instinctive almost as the bounding of a startled fawn, she jumped up and found herself in the middle of the big room, exclaiming at those amazing and familiar strangers: "What do you want?" You will note that she cried: What do you want? Not: What has happened? She told Mrs. Fyne that she had received suddenly the feeling of being personally attacked. And that must have been very terrifying. The woman before her had been the wisdom, the authority, the protection of life, security embodied and visible and undisputed.'

And this was but a foretaste of what was to follow, of the flood of vile abuse bursting from those lips that for years had uttered nothing but what was seemly and conventional. Is it surprising that a panic-terror, far more destructive and appalling than most of us experience throughout all our lives, seized upon this impressionable girl and bored its red-hot trail right through her very fibres? 'It seemed,' says Marlow, 'that poor Flora had to know all the possible phases of that sort of anguish, beginning with instinctive panic, through the bewildered stage, the frozen stage and the stage of blanched apprehension, down to the instinctive prudence of extreme terror – the stillness of the mouse.'

But observe that even in the horror of this infinitely horrifying scene, she exhibited certain inherent characteristics. When she told Mrs. Fyne how she had been called 'a little fool' over and over again – there were much worse things she had also been called – commenting 'A fool! Why, Mrs. Fyne! I do assure you I had never yet thought at all; never of anything in the world till then. And one can't be a fool without one has at least tried to think;' when she attempted to excuse Charley, of whom she had been so fond, by saying 'He at any rate had said nothing while he had looked very gloomy and miserable,' and by recalling how, at her anguished cry to him, he had dragged the governess away; and when, dumb and petrified, she had managed to scream, 'You mustn't speak like this of Papa!' on hearing the governess call him 'a cheat and a swindler,' she displayed those traits of frankness, fairness and fidelity which were instinctive. She did not pretend she had been other than a thoughtless, vapid girl; she tried to find redeeming features in the exposed wretch; she stood up for her father when she was past standing up for herself.

Of course, many other people, with quite different personalities, might have acted and thought much the same in the circumstances, but the point is that these characteristics were part of her heritage and not merely words wrung from her in distress or uttered in an effort to discover some comforting palliative. It is true that to Mrs. Fyne, bleakly kind and hospitable though she had been to Flora for years, she probably never showed more than a shadow of herself; but to begin with, there were insuperable temperamental differences between them and, secondly, both through an inevitable association of ideas and through her unhappy record of failure with her vulgar relatives and her various unsatisfactory employers, her mind had got into such a state, even to the pitch of attempting suicide, that her sensibilities were almost drowned by the hunted fright and brooding silences of a being abandoned by hope itself. Moreover, charity can be resented even while it is accepted – the poor girl had nowhere else to go to but the Fynes in the succession of catastrophes that dogged her steps – especially as she must have known that she was unpopular and that the subject of her father, now a convict, on whom all her love and compassion were centred, was a closed one. In the well-meaning, arid household of the Fynes, in which she was utterly out of place, she must have appeared angular, moody and, above all, unreceptive of Mrs. Fyne's theory that women should be able to stand up for themselves.

But she had never had a chance, and probably that occasion at Brighton when, still a child, she had rushed up effusively to Mrs. Fyne, whom she had not seen for several years, was one of the last occasions, if one excludes Charley, for many, many a long day that her feelings were uninhibited. For despite a core of courage, sometimes nearly quenched but always latent, which supported her through the hateful loneliness of her young womanhood, she was naturally unspectacular and, both from her upbringing and her character, little able to cope with life or arouse sympathy. The triumph of her malignant governess was greater than even she could have dared to expect and, with all her sense of values overturned and all her faith in herself ruined, Flora developed a kind of shrinking, sulky resentment, breeding in her distracted mind the idea that her father, another of life's victims, as she believed, was the only being in the world she had to shield. And this, as we know, led to her break with the Fynes and to her engagement to Captain Anthony.

She took particular care to drive this last fact home in her letter to Mrs. Fyne, and probably, in her rebellious mood against a fate which compelled her to rely on outside help to protect her father on his release, she convinced herself that she was taking advantage of the Captain's generous instincts, while glorying in her shamelessness. Indeed, she told Marlow long afterwards, 'I really believed I was selling myself, Mr. Marlow. And I was proud of it. What I suffered afterwards I couldn't tell you; because I only discovered my love for my poor Roderick through agonies of rage and humiliation. I came to suspect him of despising me; but I could not put it to the test because of my father. Oh! I would not have been too proud. But I had to spare Papa's feelings. Roderick was perfect, but I felt as though I were on the rack and not allowed even to cry out.'

But though she would assuredly not have married Captain Anthony had it not been for her father, equally she would not have married him unless he had profoundly entered her consciousness as a saviour of herself as well as of her parent. To quote again, 'Ever since Anthony had suddenly broken his way into her hopeless and cruel existence she lived like a person liberated from a condemned cell by a natural cataclysm, a tempest, an earthquake . . . . . . and deep down, almost unconsciously she was seduced by the feeling of being supported by this violence.'

At first, his stormy tenderness, his broken sentences flung at her like an accusation, had bedevilled and frightened her, who knew so little of men and whose mind was elsewhere; but there was that in him, an underlying gentleness and ceaseless consideration, which gradually awoke a voiceless response. 'I had already the suspicion,' guessed Marlow, 'that she did not know her own feelings. All this work of the merest chance had been so unexpected, so sudden. And she had nothing to fall back upon, no experience but such as to shake her belief in every human being.' Flora tried to be frank with Anthony, just as he tried to be frank with her, but through her diffidence and his delicacy a misunderstanding, so sundering as to make of their marriage a verbal mockery, drove them both to the verge of final despair. But can there be any real doubt that if her father had not conceived an insane hatred of his son-in-law, a hatred quite unaffected by the clear evidence of undisputed facts, all the clouds would soon have dispersed once they were together on the sea, far from the unrest and dangers and memories of the land? For despite everything she may have believed, love was stirring in her heart.

But now she was, in an ironically literal sense, between the devil and the deep sea. All day long, driving her frantic, her father kept mumbling his imprecations against her husband, and all day long Anthony, growing more silent in his baffled confusion, sought, on their joint behalf, to avoid them both as much as possible. It was not that old de Barral's words influenced her in the least, but that, having to appease him, if only negatively, an air of constraint was induced which caused Anthony to feel that they were combined against him. This, in its turn, made him more and more aloof, not pettily but through nervous strain, and made her feel that she was held in contempt for treating him so badly after all he had done for them. It was a hopeless situation, but then her life had been so full of hopeless situations that she endured it by trying to shut her mind. But even if her father had not attempted to poison Anthony (a fact never revealed to her), it is doubtful, it is very doubtful, whether she could have maintained the balance indefinitely. As she confided to Marlow, 'I did not want to hold out any longer against my own heart! I could not.' But is it not probable that, in the twilight world of the unconscious, she had been holding out against it from the beginning?

The story of Flora de Barral is made the more poignant in that Conrad did not attempt to endow her with that warm, vivid glow of personality with which he endowed such women as Mrs. Gould and Winnie Verloc, and that even in the charm of her maturity she was self-effacing and undramatic. And we may suppose that had things always gone well with her, she would still have been shy and, from a social angle, easily overlooked and underestimated. She had deep feelings, strong emotions, but it is obvious that she did not possess the immediate attraction of an impelling personality. The governess told her, in her sadistic rage, that she was 'in heart, mind, manner and appearance an utterly common and insipid creature,' and though this was a base and cruel taunt, yet it is likely enough that her lack of forcefulness, coupled with her shrinking distrust of herself, did tend to accentuate her martyrdom. What happened to her was bound to make her unsure of everything, but had she been a more assertive and robust-minded girl the effects would not have been so devastating. In fact, if she *had* been that sort of girl, the governess would probably have thought twice before employing the tactics she did.

But to visualise a specific situation calls for the visualisation of figures suitable for its development, and had Flora been other than what she was, *Chance* would be other than what it is. This does not imply any strain on credulity, it merely emphasises the need for selection. Flora lives, but she lives, so to speak, in rather subdued tones, and if we do not feel drawn to her in the same sense in which we feel drawn to some of Conrad's women characters, nevertheless we do experience real relief when she comes finally to her safe anchorage. Even in her widowhood, when time had softened memory, she is happy in the recollection of her bliss. As she said to Marlow, 'I loved and I was loved, untroubled, at peace, without remorse, without fear. All the world, all life was transformed for me.' And somehow it is pleasant to know that the unassuming, faithful Powell, who had sailed with them on so many voyages, was not to be lost to her, and that the future was secure for both of them.

RODERICK ANTHONY

TO UNDERSTAND RODERICK ANTHONY one must bear in mind, first, that his whole life had been spent at sea and that he knew next to nothing of the complexities of the land; and, secondly, that he had inherited the sensitiveness, without the brutality, of his father, the poet. Of course, these facts leave out the most important point of all, his own individuality, the thing that can play the oddest tricks with heredity, but they do shed light upon his attitude of mind and make credible what might otherwise have appeared almost incredible.

He had had practically no experience of women, and it was really an intuitive perception of the girl and her background, together with the instinctive yearning of a man of thirty-five for a mate, which caused him to fall in love with Flora de Barral. Almost instantaneously she called forth in this reticent man, so little able to express coherently the surge of his new emotions, an overwhelming sense of something that, while including pity, was much more than pity – abiding passion itself. When Marlow, talking to Flora, watched her raise her eyes and noted that it was like 'catching sight of a piece of blue sky, of a stretch of open water,' it came to him just what the look must have meant to Anthony – 'And for a moment I understood the desire of that man to whom the sea and sky of his solitary life had appeared suddenly incomplete without that glance which seemed to belong to them both.'

The eloquence which his passion aroused in this seaman so

unaccustomed to show his feelings had a tempestuous, almost convulsive, quality, as of restrained violence, which was bound to be misread by a girl who had lost all faith both in herself and in life; was bound, indeed, to alarm her as with some new menace to her already menaced existence. And the less she could cope with him, the more did his words frighten her. To her repeated, 'It's no use,' he burst out, 'No use! No use! You dare stand here and tell me that – you white-faced wisp, you wreath of mist, you little ghost of all the sorrow in the world. You dare! Haven't I been looking at you? You are all eyes. What makes your cheeks always so white, as if you had seen something? . . . Don't speak. I love it . . . No use! And you really think that I can go to sea for a year or more, to the other side of the world somewhere, leaving you behind! Why! You would vanish . . . what little there is of you. Some rough wind will blow you away altogether. You have no holding ground on earth. Well, then, trust yourself to me – to the sea – which is deep like your eyes.' Such sentences had a sort of terrifying inconsequence for the unfortunate girl thinking only of her father or of the death which would release her from despair.

This rushing torrent, coming straight from his heart, was intended to reassure her, to tell her everything at once, but even a more securely placed woman than Flora might have been intimidated at hearing such whirling words from a virtual stranger, words losing their purport in a chaos of meaningless sound; but Flora, so inured to evil, was not only intimidated, she was stunned. What fresh misfortune was this, falling on her just when she needed all her strength and resolution!

In fact, she was in such a panic that she determined on one more attempt to end everything by suicide. But again fate intervened: rising at dawn to go to the quarry, whom should she encounter in the morning twilight of the garden but Captain Anthony who, having asked her to meet him there at such an hour, a request that had not even registered, must have gained confidence from his false reading of the situation. At any rate, this meeting was the turning point, little as she had intended it to be, and he was 'gentleness itself.' His compassion and his love, so strangely and yet so touchingly expressed, began to enfold her, and though she had no trust in herself and believed she was taking advantage of his generosity, she allowed events to follow his dictated course.

Roderick Anthony was almost as friendless and lonely as was Flora de Barral, but for different reasons. Most of his time, as has been explained, was spent aboard his sailing ship; and when ashore, his distrust of life there, with 'the fads and proprieties and the ceremonies and affectations,' kept him very much to himself. And perhaps it was this, in the first instance, which drew him to be interested in the girl he met at his sister's who, though in the household, was obviously not of it. Reserved both by instinct and training, he too felt an outsider in that family circle, and this may have created a vague sort of bond. But if so, it can have lasted, metaphorically speaking, no longer than a second: suddenly, like an inspired revelation, the girl had taken complete possession of his spiritual being. Her unhappiness and desolation were more than he could bear, and if he often spoke to her in a 'fiery, masterful fashion' it was but a reflection of his inward trembling and of his longing to help.

One of the chapters of *Chance* dealing largely with Captain Anthony is headed 'The Knight,' and he was, indeed, a Knight in Shining Armour. His magnanimity, carried to the last boundary of abnegation, would appear practically unbelievable were it not that he had, of his own free will, undertaken to marry Flora in order to protect her father. When he first showed her over his ship, the *Ferndale*, before their marriage and before the release of de Barral, in a wave of insight he visualised the problems of the coming situation as he said to her, 'Your home. I can't give it to you and go away, but it is big enough for us two. You need not be afraid. If you say so I shall not even look at you. Remember that grey head of which you have been thinking night and day. Where is it going to rest? Where else if not here, where nothing evil can touch it. Don't you understand I won't let you buy shelter from me at the cost of your very soul.' And he did really mean the words. But how could it have occurred to him, or to her, that the man whose saviour he was to be would hate him with an intensity that knew no limits!

But the promise still held good, even if, in his ignorance of feminine psychology and in that kind of density which Knights in Shining Armour sometimes display, he could not perceive that it was Flora, rather than himself, who was caught in an intolerable dilemma. In his purblind heroism he was, in fact, hurting the woman he was trying to spare. But, I repeat, his promise still held good, although, being a man, he must have hoped, even if not admitting it to himself, that the conquering might of his devotion, set in the invincible medium of his own choice, would make it of no consequence. He had so counted on the sea to wipe out the misery of the past, to renovate her broken life – and all it had done, apparently, was to turn their very closeness into a bitter vacuity and to league father and daughter against him in dislike and distrust of his inescapable presence!

On shore some confidences had been exchanged, some accord had been achieved; but at sea there was nothing but the few empty words of necessary daily intercourse. The shadow of the old man, treading softly, had come between them, and Anthony's renunciation was met by a blank wall. Day by day his sense of utter failure increased upon him like some fatal disease, and 'his nervous exasperation had grown so much that now very often he used to lose control of his voice.' For, assured though he had once been, he 'had discovered that he was not the proud master but the chafing captive of his generosity.'

We may wonder why he did not insist on some explanation, however superficial, or try new tactics to draw her out, but we must never forget that, in light of his undertaking, he was too honourable to face squarely the cause of his own disillusionment. He had gambled and he had lost, and not for an instant did it enter his head that the estrangement between him and his wife might conceivably be the drag of cross purposes, each of them becoming more withdrawn as the other seemed to recede, each of them, for one reason or another, the victim of de Barral's phobia. But then, naturally, the outsider sees things coolly and in perspective, whereas Anthony's haggard thoughts gave him no peace, and, surrounded as he was by daily evidence of defeat, he had sunk into a state where his judgment ceased to be a safe guide. Powell knew that there was something wrong, 'never guessing that his young and candid eyes were in the presence of a passion profound, tyrannical and mortal, discovering its own existence, astounded at feeling itself helpless and dismayed at finding itself incurable.' Thus can the troubled and exhausted mind argue from false assumptions!

How long this tragic state of affairs could have lasted, who can tell? I suggested in my section on Flora that she might, at any time, have acted to break down the impasse; but again, deterred by her father's attitude, she might have delayed too long. Everything has its breaking point and there are undermining forces within us stronger than the strongest will. But the question was solved by de Barral's attempt to poison his son-in-law. Powell reports that, on becoming aware of this, he saw Captain Anthony 'fling his head to the right and to the left fiercely, like a wild animal at bay.' But there was no escape: this last blow to hope hammered on his brain like a thunderclap – how was he to know the origin, in its mad complications, of this dreadful act! – and it was all over. His hurried, spasmodic words to Flora, who had sensed, on her sudden appearance, the tension of the scene, have the ring of final surrender: 'I can't fight any longer for what I haven't got . . . . . . I give up . . . . . . I must learn to live without you – which I have told you was impossible. I was speaking the truth. But I have done fighting, or waiting, or hoping. Yes. You shall go.' And it was then, at last, that Flora's eyes were fully opened, that she cried out, 'You can't cast me off like this, Roderick. I won't go away from you. I won't –,' and that their imaginary chains, which can be as crippling as real chains, dropped from them. For nearly six years they sailed the seas together in complete harmony and happiness, and then just at dawn in a dense fog the *Ferndale* was cut in two by a steamer and Anthony, last to remain on board as a captain should, went down with her, though everybody else was saved. Powell, his First Mate, telling the story to Marlow four years later, wept openly. That was the kind of memory he left behind him.

It must have been a difficult task even for Conrad to breathe life into such a figure as Roderick Anthony and, by enlisting our sympathy, make him credible. For high nobility of character is an extremely hard thing to vitalise, the general tendency being to produce a picture of dummy-like and dismal worthiness. But Conrad built him up with an infinity of touches which, convincing in their cumulative effect for a reader of the novel, cannot properly be conveyed in so brief a study as this.

DE BARRAL

IT IS UNNECESSARY to waste many words on de Barral, for although he ruined thousands of people, he was, as a man, a faded, dull, stupid nonentity who, through some subconscious urge, had attached to the current catchword 'Thrift' a money-making idea and became, in consequence, a famous, and swindling, financier. But 'financier' is really too solid a word, as he was entirely ignorant and uncreative, and squandered the money that poured in upon him on the most fantastic schemes, about which he himself had only the haziest notions. In fact, he was as gullible as his dupes, and even to call him a 'swindler' would hardly represent the truth, even if, in his messianic career, he was not above faking the books in order to gain time. The old cry!

The one interesting thing about him is why this insignificant clerk, who was so unenterprising that up to then he had hardly made an effort to better his position, should suddenly have been inspired to act as he did. 'One day,' recounts Marlow, 'as though a supernatural voice had whispered into his ear or some invisible fly had stung him, he put on his hat, went out into the street and began advertising. That's absolutely all there was to it. He caught in the street the word of the time and harnessed it to his preposterous chariot.' As for being able to attract vast sums of money to himself, once he had hit upon the formula, which, according to his announcements, combined safety with ten per cent. interest, the rest was easy. In short, he had the luck to interpret the public mind just at the right moment, and in the right terms, and was 'a mere sign, a portent. There was nothing to him.'

His physical appearance exactly represented the man: 'He was clad in black. He wore a flat, broad, black satin tie in which was stuck a large cameo pin; and a small turn-down collar. His cheeks were hairless and round and apparently soft. He carried himself stiffly, walked with small steps and spoke in a gentle, inward voice.' Yes, his appearance did exactly represent him, with the exception that, beneath all his diffidence of manner, all the commonplace emptiness of his character, he had an 'overweening, unmeasurable conceit.' Natural enough, one might think, as he had risen from the humblest beginnings to great power and what seemed to be immense wealth, but somehow utterly out of keeping with his subdued, dreary personality and his unostentatious manner of life. But then there was a queer streak in him, hidden in the wordless recesses of his mind, about which nobody, including himself, knew anything. His wife, although an ineffective woman whose death caused scarcely a ripple, showed much more perspicacity than those with whom he dealt in business, being led to remark, 'I am sure he won't know what to do with all that money people are giving him to take care of for them. He's as likely as not to do something rash.' But even she never guessed the secret of the hidden de Barral. True, she rightly perceived that he was an incompetent bungler, but she had no glimpse of the subconscious urge or queer streak of which I have spoken, and apparently did not suspect that he was inordinately conceited.

But it was his overwhelming vanity, amounting to megalomania, that was his downfall, and it was this which, on his emergence from prison, made him revert almost immediately, and without even asking Flora any questions about herself, to the shameful injustice of his sentence – 'What has done for me was envy. Envy. There was a lot of them just bursting with it every time they looked my way. I was doing too well.' Again, it was this which made him receive the news of her marriage with such embittered reproaches. He was quite incapable of reading between the lines or of appreciating the sacrifice she had made on his behalf. All that he could see, or wanted to see, was that his daughter, his only child, had dared to acquire a husband when she ought to have been considering him alone. That long drive from the gaol to the docks must have been, for Flora, one of the most ghastly experiences in an existence which had known many ghastly experiences. His horrified exclamation, 'You – married? You, Flora! When? Married! What for? Who to? Married!' let loose a spate of recrimination, spoken in low-toned, vitriolic mutterings, and he even expressed the wish that he could choke her husband. And when he learnt that he was now 'Mr. Smith' and not the 'Great Mr. de Barral' it was as if a conspiracy were closing in on him.

His years in prison, during which he must have brooded incessantly over his wrongs, had carried his megalomania a step further. Flora noticed at once that there had been a change, try-ing to give it a compassionate explanation, but in truth he had become the hopeless victim of obsessions. His fixed ideas, his imperviousness to proof, his hatred of Anthony, were signs of a mental derangement arising from the basic flaw in his character which had landed him where he was.

No purpose would be served by enlarging on this and on his insane behaviour on board the *Ferndale*, for abnormal psychology is a world apart, but it can be said with the utmost assurance that the best thing old de Barral ever did was to swallow the poison he had intended for his son-in-law.

6

VICTORY

1915

LENA

UNTIL Lena met Heyst at Schomberg's hotel in the Javanese town of Samarang, she had led an unhappy and harried existence. Her mother had deserted her father, a musician playing in small theatres, when she was a little girl, and the 'landladies of various poor lodging-houses had attended casually to her abandoned childhood.' Later, after her father, who had taught her the violin, had been laid low by a paralytic stroke and taken to a home for incurables, she had drifted into Zangiacomo's Ladies' Orchestra, going with it on its tour throughout the East.

Her background could not have been more unpropitious, and her new wandering life only added to her forlornness. Mrs. Zangiacomo was actively spiteful, the other women of the orchestra were middle-aged vulgarians and, to increase her misery, the odious Schomberg had begun to make feverish advances to her. As she told Heyst early in their acquaintance, 'And I am here . . . . . . with no one to care if I make a hole in the water the next chance I get or not.'

One must understand all this to appreciate what a man like Heyst, with his courtly bearing and sympathetic, faintly humorous conversation, meant to Lena, who had never before met any one remotely resembling him. Compared with Schomberg, the 'contrast of Heyst's quiet, polished manner gave her special delight and filled her with admiration.' She was still under twenty, ignorant in some respects, experienced in others, and there was something about him, some quality at once genuine and unusual, that touched an unknown chord in her. She trusted him on his mere word, a thing which must have gone against all her training; and, though the frank artlessness of her confessions and, when he showed his friendly interest, her downright appeal for his help, may have been due to the desperate nature of her situation, in which the slightest gleam of hope had to be followed up, surely she had sensed already that instinctive bond which was, almost outside their own volition, bringing them closer together.

Indeed, between the English waif and the aristocratic Swede (it was supposed that he was a Baron) who, in his own way, was also a waif, a kind of mental link was being forged, which, when one allows for the differences of sex, age and upbringing, is the more astonishing in that it was entirely unforced. It lay deep within them, not to be explained by words, and very soon it created a feeling of inseparability which time, so disillusioning for many, could only have strengthened.

From the very first Heyst had been struck by a sort of strange contradiction in Lena. He had been 'interested by the girl's physiognomy. Its expression was neither simple nor yet very clear. It was not distinguished – that could not be expected – but the features had more fineness than those of any other feminine countenance he had ever had the opportunity to observe so closely. There was in it something indefinably audacious and infinitely miserable – because the temperament and the existence of that girl were reflected in it. But her voice! It seduced Heyst by its amazing quality . . . . . . Heyst drank in its charm as one listens to the tone of some instrument without heeding the tune.'

If her voice enthralled him, its charm gathered force from the fineness in herself which he perceived; and even if, a man of acute sensibilities, he would have pitied her in any event, it was that look of the audacious, suggestive of courage, which gave to his awakened feeling of protection the firmness of design that enabled him to act promptly and effectively. But, of course, everything would have been impossible had there not been this instinctive accord, not consciously acknowledged as yet but hovering beneath the surface, which, in the new life opening before them, threw over the whole adventure an air almost of inevitability.

Lena's nature matured very rapidly after her arrival in Samburan. When we first meet her there is a touch of the hurt and resentful child about her and, in her astonished relief at meeting Heyst, she talked without restraint. But soon, under his influence, so diffident in its affectionate solicitude, so balanced in his freedom from petulance and pettiness, the real core of her character, hidden up to now in the sordid settings of her perpetual struggle and needing only the promptings of sympathy to discover itself, emerged in its shining integrity. The more her gratitude took on the colour of devotion, the more reserved she became, partly no doubt to match his quietness in their island peace, but partly through her awareness that, though she understood him in a sense, even to his very aloofness, she did not know where she stood with him or how to pierce beyond his kind and withdrawn serenity.

The difficulties of the situation, which might have appeared insuperable, were, without strain, ignored by both of them. They had no ties with the outer world, of which they were largely ignorant, and cared not at all for its opinions. And yet neither of them was fully at ease. For Lena there was the question, Does he care for me as I care for him?, and for Heyst the problem of how to be more emotionally demonstrative so that she could see how deeply his heart was possessed by her. There was no overt shadow between them, but there was a sort of charged silence. Given time all this would have settled itself, for two people infinitely dear to one another must find a common denominator, but meanwhile their paradise was not complete. She did not dare to speak as she longed to speak, and although he had been uprooted emotionally nothing as yet could alter the fixed habit of his mind and the experiences of a lifetime. For all their proximity, for all his obvious concern for her welfare, she felt that she must do something to convince him, who had done so much for her, of her love, and thus bring about that harmony where mannerisms matter no longer because the truth behind them is itself finality. And she must do this for her own sake as well as for his.

Her chance came with the arrival, shocking in its implications, of Mr. Jones and his two companions. It came strangely and darkly, but to her feminine reason which, for all its subtle shades, seized direct upon the truth, as she saw it, it came pointed as an arrow. It was Ricardo who, prowling round to scent out the hidden treasure of Schomberg's imagination, gave her this chance. Heyst had gone out, and to her unexpected appearance in the bungalow the savage nature of the 'secretary' responded by an immediate violent attempt at assault; but being repulsed by her 'maintaining a desperate, murderous clutch on Ricardo's windpipe,' his whole attitude towards her changed, and an astonished admiration, soon to develop into an enslaved passion, took its place. She was the woman for him, she was the one to help, she was his in every fibre!

Lena, for all her suppressed panic, kept her head: devotion was stronger in her than fear. And as soon as he showed her the deadly knife with which he intended to kill Heyst, she saw at once that 'nothing stood between the enchanted dream of her

existence and a cruel catastrophe but her duplicity,' and she set
herself to wheedle it away from him. She had to deceive both
men, for only thus could she serve the man who meant everything to her and, in circumventing the enemy, justify herself and
reap her great reward: 'With a woman's frank courage, as soon
as she saw that opening she threw herself into it without reserve
. . . . . . She was appalled by the situation; but already all her
aroused femininity, understanding that whether Heyst loved
her or not she loved him, and feeling that she had brought this
on his head, faced the danger with a passionate desire to defend
her own.'

The part she had to play was like tip-toeing across a darkened
room so skilfully that no faintest tremor would be heard. In the
ardour of her over-riding idea which, woman-like, blotted out
everything else including the danger of Mr. Jones and his
revolver – but then she had not met Mr. Jones, so that, again
woman-like, such danger was only vague – the very tautness
of her mind was what was so convincing to the cunning, self-
blinded desperado. Her monosyllabic answers and scarcely-felt
touch but enhanced his conviction that, in her new loyalty and
responsive abandonment, she was casting dust in the eyes of
that ' 'yporcrit' Heyst until the moment arrived to throw off the
mask. As for Heyst himself, although at first he had suspected
that something was amiss with Lena, he was beset by so many
anxieties and the whole situation was fraught with such menace
that everything was liable to distortion, and he had to confront
the problems as they tangibly arose.

The gathering peril drew them closer together, but for her
there was the strain of the coming hour when she would get
possession of the knife and for him was the need to encourage
her by his calm. He spoke frankly to her when he had to, but

he still employed his half-playful manner. Lena, in her tortured concern for his safety, made all the more tense by the double-dealing she had to practise, felt able to speak little, and this must have seemed natural enough to Heyst. Only once did she falter, not in her determination, but in the veiled exultation that, through all the strain, bore her up. And this was when, returning from their unsuccessful mission to Wang, who, in his alarm at the intruders, would not even grant Lena and Heyst asylum, she confessed that she had been asking herself whether 'this trouble, this danger, this evil, whatever it was, finding them out in their retreat, was a sort of punishment.' Heyst, expressing his surprise, 'saw her pale face darken in the dusk. She had blushed. It was the way they lived together – that wasn't right, was it? It was a guilty life. For she had not been forced into it . . . . . . No, no – she had come to him of her own free will, with her whole soul yearning unlawfully.'

Heyst, to conceal his 'profoundly touched' feelings, which it was so necessary to conceal in the grim terrors pressing upon them, had to assume his 'best Heystian manner' to answer her – 'Are our visitors then messengers of morality, avengers of righteousness, agents of Providence? That's certainly an original view. How flattered they would be if they could only hear you!' But perceiving that she was not fully appeased by his raillery, he added, in gentle tenderness, 'Hope is a Christian virtue, and surely you can't want all the mercy for yourself.'

But this weakness, if weakness it was, soon passed, and suddenly, as if throwing off all her doubts in an inspired revival of her exultation, she cried, 'I don't care. I would do more yet! And some day you'll forgive me. You'll have to forgive me!' It was on such terms, intimate and yet, in a sense, secret and at cross purposes, that they awaited the hour which was to bring

Heyst's last and momentous visit to Mr. Jones, the visit from which he scarcely expected to return alive. But his strict injunctions that, on his departure, she was to escape into the forest to return only on his giving a specified signal or, if he gave none, to go to Wang and beg him – surely alone and in the circumstances he would not now refuse her – for protection, passed unheeded by the girl, intent on her own plan and whose hour of decision was also approaching. She must meet Ricardo while Heyst was with his master, she must get the knife from him!

The scene of her effort, carried on in the lit bungalow amid the crash and mutterings of a tropical thunderstorm, has an air of breathless climax, in which her victory, so complete and so pitiful, is the very prelude to her death. It is in the true manner of great tragedy, and the language describing it has a poetry of its own which flows from Conrad's creative imagination with a rare intensity. In that laden atmosphere what could match the tone of the words in which her triumph on being handed the knife are envisaged? 'At the moment when she bent forward to receive it from him, there was a flash of fire in her mysterious eyes – a red gleam in the white mist which wrapped the promptings and longings of her soul. She had done it! The very sting of death was in her hands; the venom of the viper in her paradise, extracted, safe in her possession.'

But, as we know, Ricardo's escapade had been discovered by Mr. Jones, who was conscious at once that it was the end of their association, and the shot intended for him only grazed his cheek to pierce the girl's breast. (Many readers, I fancy, believe that the shot was meant for Lena, but what is said on a subsequent page disproves this.) She did not realise that she had been hit, her thoughts and her looks were all for Heyst, now at her side again: ' "I knew you would come back in time! You are safe

now. I have done it! I would never, never have let him —."
Her voice died out, while her eyes shone on him as when the sun
breaks through a mist. "Never get it back. Oh, my beloved." '

Heyst, still horribly deluded that she had betrayed him for
Ricardo, answered with a quiet bitterness hardly disguised by his
habitual courtesy, but fortunately she misunderstood and merely
supposed that, as usual, he was mildly poking fun at her. All
the same, she had earned more than that: 'The exultation vanished from her face. "You mustn't make fun of me now. I know
no shame. I was thanking God with all my sinful heart for having
been able to do it – for giving you to me in that way – oh, my
beloved – all my own at last!" ' Then, indeed, he understood.

The life of the poor girl, so justified in her victory, was ebbing
away, but her final words upheld her in the ecstasy of her self-
sacrifice for the man she so truly loved: ' "Who else could have
done this for you?" she whispered gloriously. "No one in the
world," he answered her in a murmur of unconcealed despair.'
And thus, 'with that divine radiance on her lips she breathed
her last, triumphant, seeking for his glance in the shades of
death.'

Lena is assuredly one of Conrad's most touching women
characters, and Conrad himself seems to have been of this
opinion, for it was from *Victory* he read extracts on the only
occasion on which he gave a reading in semi-public, which was
in New York in May 1923. As he wrote me at the time, 'I gave
a talk and readings from *Victory*. One hour and a quarter with
an ovation at the end. They were most attentive. Laughs at
proper places and snuffles at the last when I read the whole
chapter of Lena's death.' And yet, enchanting as Lena is, with an
effortless power to bring men to her feet, we never see her very
clearly, as if somehow she had been enveloped in a gauzy haze.

Is it perhaps that she is the supreme example of a 'one-man' woman, so supreme that even the reader is kept out of the secret; and would she have blossomed as beautifully, however favourable the setting, in the world of people as in the seclusion of Samburan, where she had a single human being all to herself?

HEYST

W<small>HILE IT IS RIGHT THAT</small> L<small>ENA</small>, whose act of heroic sacrifice gives the title to this book, should come first in a study of its
characters, it is a question whether Axel Heyst, in the remarkable
integration of his personality, is not an even more interesting
figure. The natural tendency of his mind, fortified by the teach-
ings of his father, made him an observer of life rather than an
active participator in it, and his intellectual aloofness was such
that he had no close friends and concerned himself as little as
possible with what was going on around him. All this was so out
of keeping with the attitude expected of a white man in the
East, especially of a white man who was not eccentric in such
relations as he had, that he received such nicknames as 'Enchanted Heyst,' 'Utopist Heyst' and so on which, in such a
society, were sure indications that he was considered odd in a
rather inexplicable way. 'For fifteen years' we are told 'Heyst
had wandered, invariably courteous and unapproachable, and in
return was generally considered a "queer chap." He had started
off on these travels of his after the death of his father, an ex-
patriated Swede who died in London, dissatisfied with his
country and angry with all the world, which had instinctively
rejected his wisdom.'

Heyst tried to explain to the mystified Lena that he was what
he was owing to the influence of his father: 'It was as if that mind
were taking me into its confidence, giving me a special insight
into its mastery of despair . . . . . . After listening to him I could

not take my soul down into the street to fight there. I started to wander about, an independent spectator – if that is possible.' Later in the same conversation he added, 'I am not for nothing the son of my father . . . . . . I am he, all but the genius. And there is even less in me than I make out, because the very scorn is falling away from me year after year.' But assuredly, though he had imbibed from his father's books and talk a scornful sense of the general futility of things, disguised under a reserved bearing and as free of rancour as it was of enthusiasm, he was more sensitive and less dogmatic than his parent; and he possessed, of his own right, an unexplored fund of humanity and an unknown passion of feeling, which, when called upon, startled him by their fullness and revealed depths in himself of which he was so ignorant and sceptical that, though he could face them practically, he could not overcome his diffidence.

Without being a hermit, Heyst had a 'taste for solitude,' and had it not been for Morrison – to whose assistance he had come at a critical moment and who, in his gratitude, had insisted, all against his benefactor's secret wishes, on giving him an interest in the Tropical Coal Belt Company he was then projecting – it is probable that he would have continued to wander about the East, gathering facts and impressions and fastidiously indifferent, under his perfect manners, to the people he met and the events he watched. He had just sufficient private means to do what he wanted in a small way, and although he became the manager in the East for the coal company, which collapsed almost before it was born, it was, as I have said, more to please Morrison, whom he could not bear to disappoint, than to assure himself a definite purpose in life.

The company's business was established in Samburan, an island, perhaps one of the Tiger Islands, which Conrad informed me was presumed to lie off the south coast of Celebes, and after the company went into liquidation Heyst continued to live in the managerial bungalow with one Chinese servant, quite negatively content to revert to his independent and solitary existence. Every ten days an acquaintance of his, Captain David-son, the master of a merchant steamer, used to pass close enough inshore on his regular run to watch for any signal the marooned Heyst might care to give. It was of his own volition he per-formed this kindly act, but he 'could not possibly guess that Heyst, alone on the island, felt neither more nor less lonely than in any other place, desert or populous. Davidson's concern was, if one may express it so, the danger of spiritual starvation; but this was a spirit which had renounced all outside nourishment, and was sustaining itself proudly on its own contempt of the usual coarse aliments which life offers to the common appetites of men.'

People such as Heyst do exist, but usually in a much modified guise. He was not anti-social, he was always friendly, but he was quite able to live a balanced life in the peopled solitude of his own thoughts. Having never done anyone a conscious wrong and being utterly without ambition, he had nothing to regret; but ironically enough it was the financial aid he had rendered Morrison, saving his brig from being sold for a song by the Portuguese in Timor, that enabled Schomberg to vent his idiotic hate upon him by making out that he had swindled Morrison and been the cause of his death in England. Schomberg's abys-mal stupidity was only matched by his pointless malice, but Heyst remained so totally unaware of all this that it was to his hotel he still went on his occasional visits to Samarang.

It was on one of those visits that he met Lena through the mere chance of listening to a concert given by the Ladies'

Orchestra of which she was a member and chatting to her afterwards. Heyst was not an impressionable man, in the special meaning implied, nor was he in the least interested in amorous adventure, but through an extraordinary concatenation of circumstances and impressions, overwhelming in their ultimate force, he found himself set to rescue Lena from a predicament miserable at the time and hopeless for the future. But the whole thing compressed to a point was much more than an act of compassion, it was an awakened bell sounding in his heart.

It might have been supposed that Heyst, of all men, was the least likely to be so carried off his balance as to undertake a precipitate and desperate act, the outcome of which threatened to upset the whole scheme of his existence that, now in his middle-thirties, had become, as he believed, completely set. But this would be to judge him by what he had made of his life hitherto rather than by what was tacit in his freedom from inhibitions and his mastery of his own destiny. He was not the slave of preconceived ideas except along general lines, and if he had hitherto done nothing spectacular, it was simply because nothing had seemed worthwile: 'Those dreamy spectators of the world's agitation,' as Conrad puts it, 'are terrible once the desire to act gets hold of them. They lower their heads and charge a wall with an amazing serenity which nothing but an indisciplined imagination can give.'

Heyst's uniform composure, which had a certain touch of old-fashioned primness about it, was always absolutely under control – even when rescuing Morrison, whose despair at such sudden disaster had unloosed an emotional flood, his measured words, 'I would be very happy if you would allow me to be of use,' came quite naturally, despite his profound pity – and this composure, tactfully delicate and charmingly playful, still per-

sisted when, with resolute planning and action, he had snatched
Lena from the hotel and carried her off with him to Samburan.
His feelings were deeply engaged, he left nothing to chance, but
the Heyst who had long been regarded as slightly peculiar could
not change his manner or allow his feelings free play.

But indeed it was, as we know, just this manner of his which,
in her helpless, forsaken state, appealed so much to Lena when
she first met him, as if, surrounded as she was by a repellent
throng, his sympathetic politeness had all the magic of unbelievable contrast. When, for instance, he prompted her to
smile to delude Schomberg, who was sitting at a nearby table,
and she told him later 'I've not had many chances to smile in my
life,' only to get the response, 'but you do it most charmingly –
in a perfectly fascinating way . . . . . . it went as straight to my
heart as though you had smiled for the purpose of dazzling me,'
is it surprising that the girl's voice in answering him was 'un-
steady, gentle, and incredulous?' Certainly he had wanted to
soothe and encourage her, but for the life of him he could not
have spoken thus unless it was the truth – and truth can shine
through the simplest of words. Never before had any man
addressed her in such a tone or given her such a feeling of safety.

One sees Heyst vividly, but it is much easier to see him than to
describe him, for it is extremely difficult to get past the smooth
surface of his exterior. Amiable and unassertive, sensitive, silent
and faintly disdainful, he went on his self-effacing way without
anybody really knowing more about him than conjecture might
suggest. To Lena he referred to himself as the 'most detached of
creatures in this earthly activity, the veriest tramp on this earth,
an indifferent stroller going through the world's bustle;' but his
unruffled behaviour which, without being stiff, kept people at
arm's length – even Davidson, who liked him and whose direct

simplicity appealed to Heyst, admitted that 'he isn't the sort of man one can speak familiarly to ' – hid a side of his nature which hitherto his distrust of life and his command of himself had screened. But now that this side had emerged, he found, I repeat, that he could not rid himself of his ingrained mental equipment.

Heyst's outward composure did not desert him when the vile trio of 'Plain Mr. Jones,' Ricardo and the ape-like Pedro descended upon Samburan, and his inward dismay was all for Lena. Being invariably himself in his polished reserve, he scarcely pretended, even to begin with, that they were harmless castaways, and being totally fearless he did not attempt to assuage them. In fact, it was his calm demeanour, tinged with contempt, which gave them the idea that he was excessively 'deep' and that the treasure he was supposed to possess must be hidden with extreme care. Thus, also believing him to be armed, resolute and quite incapable of being frightened, they went about their business of robbing and, no doubt, finally murdering him with a finesse quite alien to their usually brutally direct methods, although the corrupt soul of 'Plain Mr. Jones,' avaricious as it was, did find satisfaction in the cat-and-mouse game he had to play.

Heyst was, indeed, under no delusions about them. He soon perceived that Mr. Jones, the head and brains of the gang, 'was an absolutely hard and pitiless scoundrel' who, even had he been able to convince him that the story of his wealth was only a fiction, would not have spared him; but he still maintained his detached and scornful attitude and, so far as his own security was concerned, was totally unimpressed by the revelation of infinite evil and hidden threats which emanated from the spectral Jones. For example, when the wretch, made suddenly aware that he was being double-crossed by Ricardo, tried to call a truce with

Heyst, he 'wearily' replied, 'Have I been making war on you?
...... How do you expect me to attach any meaning to your
words? ...... You seem to be a morbid, senseless sort of bandit.
We don't speak the same language.' In truth, he talked to him
as if he had been no more than a petty thief whom he had found
trying to pick his pocket.

But all the same he appreciated only too clearly the frightful
danger Lena and himself were in from these menacing cut-
throats, particularly now that his Chinese servant Wang had
stolen his revolver and deserted his service; but his frame of
mind, especially since Lena had told him of the Schomberg cal-
umny, was such that a feeling of utter disgust was what affected
him most. As he said to her after her first sight of them, 'You
have seen them now ...... Think what it was to me to see them
land in the dusk, fantasms from the sea – apparitions, chimæras!
And they persist. That's the worst of it – they persist. They have
no right to be – but they are. They ought to have aroused my
fury. But I have refined everything away by this time – anger,
indignation, scorn itself. Nothing's left but disgust.'

Yet all such thoughts were but a backwash from his old self
brought face to face with the likelihood of losing, at its very
outset, the marvellous new life opening about him. If mistrust of
everything was again pressing on his mind, it was a sort of pain
which still held close to his heart the precious dearness of Lena's
presence: 'Every time she spoke she seemed to abandon to him
something of herself – something excessively subtle and inex-
pressible, to which he was infinitely sensible, which he would
have missed horribly if she were to go away.' This was the
Heyst who, through all his renewed distrust of emotion, took
every precaution that was possible by carefully detailed instruc-
tions to save his paradise by saving Lena. For even if he himself

were doomed, which he suspected, the woman who had made his paradise must be saved, if saved she could be.

We know that fate intervened to ruin everything, but even had they come together again in the bliss of a recovery from incalculable peril, Heyst would still have remained the victim of his temperament, of his upbringing, of the twisted wisdom that had been instilled into him – remained the victim, that is to say, until the dawned light in her finally threw its invincible reflection over him, just as he remained the victim of it even when Lena lay dying. She was the whole world to him, every drop in his veins was hers, but when she whisperingly asked, 'Why don't you take me into your arms and carry me out of this lonely place?', all he could do was to bend 'low over her, cursing his fastidious soul, which even at that moment kept the true cry of love from his lips in its infernal distrust of all life.' A minute later, admittedly, as at her final breath he put his arm under her, all at once the demon, with its restraining hand, was exorcised and he was 'ready to lift her up in his firm arms and take her into the sanctuary of his innermost heart – for ever!' – but would it have been exorcised had not death been standing at his elbow?

Almost the last words Heyst spoke to Davidson, who, learning the initial story from Mrs. Schomberg, had turned on his tracks in the middle of a trip to hurry to Samburan, were, 'Ah, Davidson, woe to the man whose heart has not learnt while young to hope, to love – and to put its trust in life!' Then left alone with his dead, he threw himself into the fire he had kindled for them both.

'PLAIN MR. JONES'

WHATEVER 'Plain Mr. Jones's' real name may have been, it was assuredly not one to which he did any credit. Indeed, in the gallery of Conrad's evil characters, he stands out as perhaps the most depraved of all, living off the weaknesses and vices of others, utterly cold-blooded and cruel, and with a decadent streak in him horrible in its intensity and irrelevance. He evidently belonged to a good family, even if 'gentleman' was a word to be complacently mentioned rather than lived up to, but his past had obviously been infamous, as it was when fleeing from England in a ship chartered by treasure-seekers, as Ricardo confided in Heyst, that he had first met him. According to his own explanation to Heyst, prefaced by the portentous but unfinished sentence, 'I am he who is –,' having 'refused to conform to certain usual conventions, he was a rebel now, and was coming and going up and down the earth.'

It would be a mistake, however, to think that he was in any sense excusing himself, for he was one of those born criminals, with a frozen expression and an abominable ruthlessness, who are the outcasts of a society they both hate and despise. He had his fits of lethargy and boredom which Ricardo dreaded, but generally speaking he was determined and alert and went on his way leaving a trail of misery behind him. And from the moment he enters this story, espied by Schomberg with his 'dark, sunken stare plunging down on him over the rail of the first-class part of the deck,' disaster follows close upon the shadow of his long, lanky, ageing figure.

Mr. Jones's ostensible profession was that of card-sharper, but this is a mild way of describing his activities. Terrorism, in one form or another, terrorism not stopping short of murder, was the equipment with which he faced existence. And he was remarkably competent at his job, although as, in the nature of things, he had to be constantly on the move, his financial status seems to have been perpetually precarious. But if he was bent on grabbing all the money he could, what appealed to him even more was the thrill of getting some nervous weakling into his toils. He was, indeed, steeped in such an air of rottenness that it was, as one might say, almost physically perceptible, like a foul odour.

To some extent this was created by his appearance, with its 'used-up, weary, depraved distinction' and its 'curious character of evil,' and to some extent by his conversation with its casually dreadful admissions, as when he remarked 'languidly, and in a voice indifferent, as if issuing from a tomb, that he depended on himself, as if the world was still one great, wild jungle without law;' but it reached beyond that, as though, through the intensity of his imagination, Conrad had conjured up, in the guise of a mortal, an emanation of corruption itself. Wherever Mr. Jones went, his aura went with him, tainting the atmosphere, and it is no wonder that he alarmed Schomberg as much as he disgusted Heyst. For it was not alone what he looked like, what he said, what he did, it was what he *was*.

Mr. Jones's morbid horror of women, as if merely to see one was like a touch of disease, adds to the macabre picture and differentiates him still more from the normal sanity of life. The contrast between his nervous outbursts at even hearing about a woman and his contemptuous callousness in discussing his own atrocious deeds is repulsive to such a pitch as almost to suggest a man one side of whose face is that of a blubbering idiot and the other side that of a sneering fiend. When, for instance, he is informed by Heyst of Lena's presence on Samburan, 'the whole man seemed frozen still. "Here! Here!" he screamed out twice. There was no mistaking his astonishment, his shocked in-credulity – something like frightened disgust;' whereas when, hardly having met Schomberg, he answers, in reply to a request for their names to enter in the hotel register, 'My name? Oh, plain Mr. Jones – put that down – a gentleman at large. And this is Ricardo . . . . . . You don't want any more of our history, do you? Eh, what? Occupation? Put down – well, tourists. We've been called harder names before now; it won't hurt our feelings. And that fellow of mine . . . . . . He's Peter. Citizen of Colombia . . . . . . Pedro, alligator-hunter . . . . . . Shall I tell you how I killed his brother in the wilds of Colombia? Well, perhaps some other time – it's a rather long story. What I shall always regret is that I didn't kill him, too. I could have done it without any extra trouble then; now it's too late.'

It is true that Heyst's news about Lena suddenly opened his eyes to the real facts and he knew at once that he had been double-crossed; but his abhorrence at the thought of a woman's presence nearby was exactly what he had expressed on various more innocuous occasions: in its morbid perversity it only makes 'Plain Mr. Jones' more disgusting than ever. But within his limits he was certainly very intelligent. The mere fact of Lena's existence on the island explained everything in a flash, unbaring the whole elaborate deception of which he had been the victim. He knew immediately from the accumulation of hints that he could no longer trust his former 'secretary,' and he also knew just what that meant. Mr. Jones and Ricardo spoke the same language where matters of self-interest were concerned, and for the last four years their views had been identical. As Conrad says, 'There was a similarity of mind between these two – one the outcast of his vices, the other inspired by a spirit of scornful defiance, the aggressiveness of a beast of prey looking upon all the tame creatures of the earth as its natural victims.' But now that the image of a woman, a conquering woman, had risen between these two wretches whose instincts had hitherto been to hunt as a pair, it spelt death for one or the other. First come, first served! Mr. Jones had almost been caught napping, but Ricardo, for all his cunning, was not his match once the position had been summed up. For he had the swift intelligence to perceive not only that his hold on Ricardo had gone for ever, but that his former henchman was planning to kill him – which was quite accurate. For Ricardo had thrown off his allegiance for ever and he was not going to allow Mr. Jones to stand in his way.

Mr. Jones had also appreciated at first sight that Heyst was not at all the type of man he could bully, as, for example, he could bully Schomberg, in whom 'the spectral intensity of that glance, fixed on the hotel-keeper (and this was most frightful), without any definite expression, seemed to dissolve the last grain of resolution in his character.' Mr. Jones's spectre-like appearance, to which reference is frequently made, was in fact part of his stock-in-trade, but as it was not assumed simply to frighten, it *did* frighten, for behind it lurked the mirror of his remorseless soul. But Heyst, who was as completely master of himself as any man ever was, was quite unimpressed and quite uncowed when faced by this man whose clear purpose was rapine and murder. 'He seems to be a very self-possessed man,' said Mr.

Jones to Ricardo; and again, 'We haven't to do with a young fool that can be led on by chaff or flattery, and in the end simply overawed. This is a calculating man.' He did not admire Heyst for this, any more than he felt gratitude because he had saved him and his followers from dying of thirst, but it gave ground for thought. 'This thing, Martin,' he observed later, 'is not like our other tries. I have a peculiar feeling about this. It's a different thing. It's a sort of test.'

It *was* a different thing. Both Mr. Jones and Ricardo had come on a fool's errand, for there was no plunder to be got, and Mr. Jones was doubly fooled because Ricardo had found what he believed to be a more priceless treasure than loot and, in doing so, had also been doubly fooled. Never before were two such blood-thirsty and avaricious ruffians misled so completely by their own desires. But the taste of death lay all around, and Mr. Jones's amusement at playing with his foredoomed victim and Ricardo's ecstasy at meeting with his ordained woman could take neither its flavour nor its reality out of the circumambient air.

Every time one tries to get at grips with Mr. Jones in an effort to discover what actuated him, he eludes one's enquiries because, for all his pulsing sense of being, there is something nightmarish about him, as if he had been spewed up from the very dregs of the underworld. In reading his various conversations with Heyst, in which he is constantly mentioning that he may have to murder or maim him, his manner of speech, as from one gentleman to another, is peculiarly atrocious, and the difference between his drawled, mincing words and his sharp, icy, veno-mous eyes has the sickening quality of unutterable viciousness. 'How do you define yourself?' asks Heyst, only to be answered, 'I, my dear sir? In one way I am – yes, I am the world itself, come to pay you a visit. In another sense I am an outcast – almost an

[242]

outlaw. If you prefer a less materialistic view, I am a sort of fate – the retribution that waits its time.'

How far 'Plain Mr. Jones' was completely sane at any period is a question, but towards the end of the book he seems to have gone really mad. As he prepared to shoot Ricardo – the shot which, alas, killed Lena – the 'crazy bandit jabbered thinly' into Heyst's ear, 'Behold the simple Acis kissing the sandals of the nymph . . . . . . while the menacing pipe of Polyphemus sounds close at hand – if he could only hear it!'

The last glimpse we are vouchsafed of Mr. Jones comes through the placid words of Davidson speaking to the Dutch Excellency who wanted to hear all details about the tragedy on Samburan that had created such a stir: 'I suppose he tumbled into the water by accident – or perhaps not by accident. The boat and the man were gone' – by this time, of course, Mr. Jones had shot Ricardo, and Wang, Heyst's Chinese servant, had shot Pedro and cut the boat loose – 'and the scoundrel saw himself all alone, his game clearly up, and fairly trapped. Who knows? The water's very clear there, and I could see him huddled up on the bottom between two piles, like a heap of bones in a blue silk bag, with only the head and the feet sticking out.'

And as the sea went to work upon him, let us hope that it washed away, with his body, the very memory of his darkened life.

RICARDO

IN CERTAIN RESPECTS Ricardo's mind was so complementary to that of 'Plain Mr. Jones' that no word was necessary for a complete understanding between them. As Ricardo remarked to Schomberg, 'He just beckoned to me, and that was enough.' Both of them were, by instinct, savage iconoclasts, anti-social to the last degree, and totally devoid of the emotions which influence the lives of most people, such as pity, remorse, decency or conscience. But even allowing for their similarity of outlook, it may be doubted whether their partnership would have lasted as long as it did, had not Ricardo developed an exaggerated regard, not however without a slightly amused superiority, for what a 'gentleman' was and had come to consider Mr. Jones as the very epitome of his ideal. As he said to Schomberg, 'I should know one drunk, in the gutter, in jail, under the gallows. There's something – it isn't exactly the appearance, it's a – no use my trying to tell you.'

This regard had, of course, nothing whatsoever to do with any conventional interpretation of conduct, but only with certain externals of behaviour which, being different from his own, had come to be accepted with a sort of admiring wonder as a thing that could not be learnt but was inherently a matter of class. It was not that he wanted to be a gentleman, for he was profoundly satisfied with his own personality and position, but that it added a kind of zest to his predatory nature to know that even the most remarkable of this incomprehensible breed was also as predatory and as unscrupulous as himself.

In appearance Ricardo bore no resemblance to his master. He was a 'muscular, short man with eyes that gleamed and blinked, a harsh voice, and a round, toneless, pock-marked face ornamented by a thin, dishevelled moustache sticking out quaintly under the tip of a rigid nose.' But even Schomberg, who was not an acute psychologist, perceived before very long that 'these two were indeed well matched in their enormous dissimilarity, identical souls in different disguises.' His judgment was correct, and yet the tie, close as it appeared to be, was precarious in its very essence, for not only, as we are told, is there no honour among thieves, but beasts of prey are wrapped up in themselves and men who live by violence are not safe companions.

Ricardo was as cynically frank, when in the mood, as was Mr. Jones – with both of them such frankness was not only native to their arrogant attitude, but a calculated method of intimidating others – and in the long conversation, covering nearly three chapters, which he had with Schomberg, he reduced the wretched hotel keeper to a state bordering on panic. And yet he was in a surprisingly affable frame of mind: 'An unsuspected stream of loquacity had broken its dam somewhere deep within the man, had diluted his fiery blood and softened his pitiless fibre. Schomberg experienced mingled relief and apprehension, as if suddenly an enormous savage cat had begun to wind itself about his legs in inexplicable friendliness. No prudent man under such circumstances would dare to stir. Schomberg didn't stir.' No, he kept as quiet as possible and had to listen to the grisly story of Ricardo's adventures with Mr. Jones and of their relationship to society.

Murder meant nothing to him – throughout the book he

constantly reverts to the desirability of 'plugging' with a re-revolver or 'ripping up' with a knife – and his genial conversation on the subject with Schomberg made the other's blood run cold. For example, 'Once I was courting a girl. I used to kiss her behind the ear and say to myself: "If only you knew who's kissing you, my dear, you would scream and bolt!" ' So who can say who he really was ? – for 'Ricardo' by itself is no more revealing than 'Mr. Jones,' though perhaps a notorious and particularly ghastly murderer would not be far wrong. And how he came to be mate of the schooner in which he met Mr. Jones is another mystery, though he was a sailor by profession; but then we know nothing of the background of either man, even if it be permissible to surmise a great deal from their own hints.

For all his strength, Ricardo could move as silently as a hunting animal, and if Schomberg did feel that his unexpected affability resembled that of a 'savage cat' in a queer friendly mood, he was pretty close to the mark. For instance, when, unknown to Heyst, Ricardo was talking to Lena in the bungalow and all at once heard the voice of the returned Swede, he was 'on his feet in an instant, as noiseless as a cat. His yellow eyes gleamed, gliding here and there; but he, too, seemed unable to make another movement. Only his moustache stirred visibly, like the feelers of some animal.' Or again, when he was trying to convince Heyst that sending Pedro to the boat was 'on the level' and the other did not reply, 'his eyes glided voluptuously here and there, cruel and dreamy,' rather as one may see a cat's eyes glide vacantly and stonily about a room.

Such glimpses suggest a formidable ruthlessness, and Ricardo was, in truth, as formidable and ruthless as Mr. Jones. Also, though elementary and, indeed, elemental in his instincts, with a passionate resentment against everybody and everything that was 'tame' (a very favourite word with him) and a simple method of solving troublesome problems, he was an exceedingly crafty man, completely self-assured and able to act with a sort of fraudulently open heartiness that must have deceived many. It even deceived Mr. Jones, who knew his henchman well, when he managed to conceal from him Lena's presence on Samburan, until Heyst found that he, himself, had to reveal it. At first, knowing his master's horror of women, he had thought it better policy for the success of their plan to keep the knowledge to himself; but later, when he had fallen head over ears in love with the girl, he resolved to continue this silence until he could catch his 'gentleman' unawares and kill him with the knife that was always strapped to his leg.

That a rapacious brute like Ricardo could have got himself so hopelessly, one might almost say so lyrically, enmeshed with any woman may seem incredible. But there is no telling what may happen to a man, even to a man much less virile and adventurous than he was, when passion, in its incalculable manifestations, gets the upper hand. He started out to rape or murder and he ended by adoring, which does not in the least imply that the tiger had turned into a dove. As Conrad says, 'His passions being thoroughly aroused, a thirst for blood was allied in him with a thirst for tenderness – yes, tenderness. A sort of anxious, melting sensation pervaded and softened his heart when he thought of that girl – one of his own sort. And at the same time jealousy started gnawing at his breast as the image of Heyst intruded itself on his fierce anticipation of bliss.'

In his besotted infatuation, reinforced by his belief in his invincibility, he was persuaded that Lena had been entirely won over, but even so he was overwhelmed by the very intensity of his emotions: ' "I am dog tired" he said, and sat down on the floor. "I went tired this morning, since I came in here and started talking to you – as tired as if I had been pouring my life-blood here on these planks for you to dabble your white feet in;" ' and later in the conversation, 'We'll go on wandering the world over, you and I, both free and both true. You are no cage bird. We'll rove together, for we are of them that have no homes. We are born rovers.' Such sentences have, in themselves, the note of authenticity, but whether Ricardo, an illiterate man, would have uttered them seems somehow doubtful – though there again, who has fathomed the transmuting power of passion?

Ricardo was playing a dangerous game, balanced between Heyst and Mr. Jones, with, as he fondly supposed, Lena as the prize, once he had dealt in his usual efficient manner with the two men. But his nerves were wearing thin, and the tension in the bungalow on the night, obviously the critical night for all of them, when he dined with Lena and Heyst was almost un- bearable. 'The air,' as Conrad describes it, 'seemed to grow more oppressive with every word spoken,' and, 'for some time all three had given up any pretence of eating.' Lena, absorbed in her scheme for getting the knife, scarcely spoke; Heyst was, as ever, contemptuously brief in his responses to Ricardo; and for all Ricardo's forced chatter, he could hardly keep his hands off his host and could not altogether restrain the 'hidden venom' of his language: 'H'm! One can see . . . . . . that you are a gentle- man,' spurts from him, 'but all that gentlemanly fancifulness is apt to turn sour on a plain man's stomach.'

It was extremely ominous and menacing, with storm brewing in every heart, and the elements, as if sharing in the sense of fatality, beginning to rumble in the oncome of a tempest; and to Heyst's observation, as he walked away with Ricardo for his final talk with Mr. Jones, that the weather symptoms might end in nothing, Ricardo's 'vicious' rejoinder, 'No! Let it come! ......I am in the humour for it!' was an obvious indication of how near he was to breaking point and of how this slave of love longed to savour the taste of death in the same hour as he savoured the taste of life.

Ricardo is an easier person to understand than is Mr. Jones in that, for all his frightfulness, he was more normal. Allowing for his delirium, he is all of a piece, ruthless, cunning, and as devoid of compassion as a scorpion – which also carries a deadly weapon. But, of course, 'normal' is a relative word, and as we happen to live in a communal society, Ricardo's theory that mankind existed solely for the purpose of being plundered and that human life was the merest trifle, suggests that, in a more comprehensive interpretation of sanity, he was a criminal degenerate who ought to have been locked up in his youth for ever.

SCHOMBERG

IF IT WERE NOT THAT Schomberg's habit of scandal-mongering lay at the root of all the tragedy in *Victory*, he would scarcely be worth a section to himself, so second-rate and contemptible is he in his posturing emptiness. He appears in several of Conrad's works, always running an hotel and a table d'hôte in one part or another of the East, and always ready to gossip and embroider stories; but though he was completely unreliable, despite his 'austere Lieutenant-of-the-Reserve manner,' yet he managed to make his personality felt and to do far more harm than even he could have contemplated. Indeed, being a coward, and an infatuated coward at that, he would never have dared to set going what he did set going had he visualised the consequences.

For some reason, perhaps because he did not patronise his hotel sufficiently, perhaps because of his uncommunicative, detached behaviour, Heyst had always been detested by Schomberg, and when the ill-starred Morrison, whom Heyst had saved from ruin, died unexpectedly in Europe, the hotel keeper, as I have said previously, saw his chance and announced weightily, 'That's what comes of having anything to do with that fellow. He squeezes you dry like a lemon, then chucks you out – sends you home to die.' Such envenomed spite, based more likely on instinctive elaboration of bare facts than on intentional lying, grows with time, and gradually his hate became a kind of mania with the Teutonic Schomberg, whose perpetual stream of underhand abuse, while laughed at by those who knew Heyst, did inevitably produce some sort of effect on strangers, as we learn from Lena's own lips.

It is true that he did have his hour of triumph when the Tropical Coal Belt Company, of which Heyst had been appointed manager in the East, went smash. All the sailing captains, who formed such a large part of Schomberg's clientele, had felt sure that its promising start spelt their ruin; but Schomberg had always prophesied its failure, remarking dogmatically, 'All this is very well, gentlemen; but he can't throw his coal-dust in my eyes. There's nothing in it. Why, there can't be anything in it. A fellow like that for manager?' This justified verdict, not based on knowledge but on 'imbecile hatred, or mere stupid tenacity of opinion,' must have brought him a good deal of prestige, but though he continued to bore people by an occasional outburst against Heyst, now living alone on Samburan, where once everything had been bustle and activity, the Swede no longer counted at all and was virtually forgotten.

One can imagine therefore what it meant to Schomberg when Lena, the only young and attractive woman, the only Englishwoman, indeed, in the fantastic Zangiacomo's Ladies' Orchestra, then staying at his hotel, with whom he had fallen completely in love, ran off with the hated and despised Heyst! He had felt so sure of his triumph – even 'the aversion she showed him as far as she dared (for it is not always safe for the helpless to display the delicacy of their sentiments), Schomberg pardoned on the score of feminine conventional silliness' – that he was 'rather pleased than otherwise' to observe that Heyst, who had come over from his island on business for a few days, was chatting with the girl, as 'the silly fellow would keep everybody else off.' Self-delusion is not uncommon, and the man he was soon to refer to as a 'vagabond, impostor, swindler, ruffian, *schwein-*

hund!' was now, to his besotted complacency, a merely ridiculous figure. For wasn't everything going just as he wanted it
to go?

Schomberg was forty-five, a dangerous age for a man, particularly a man who loathed his wife as much as he loathed Mrs.
Schomberg, a mouse-like, shrinking creature but far more
astute and determined than he ever guessed. He kept pressing
his attentions on the girl when he could get her alone for a
moment 'in quiet corners and empty passages' with a frantic
abandon that stopped at nothing and insultingly took for granted
that he was only expressing her own wishes. Here is the sort of
thing: 'We'll soon get rid of the old woman . . . . . . Hang her!
I've never cared for her. The climate don't suit her; I shall tell
her to go to her people in Europe. She will have to go, too! I will
see to it. *Eins, zwei,* march! And then we shall sell this hotel and
start another somewhere else.' The harassed Lena, stunned by the
urgent violence of the whispered words, was beside herself with
disgust and fear. Already utterly desolate in her forlorn situation, she abhorred this beast of a man, creepingly alert to snatch
his chance of panted declarations, and it was her awful sense of
being hemmed in on every side that made her so ready to confide
in such an utterly different type of man as Heyst.

And yet there is no doubt that, in his ravings, tremulous with
desire, Schomberg was expressing a kind of slobbering sincerity,
even in the very vileness of his remarks. He really was 'hard hit,'
as the saying is, and with the egotism of the ruthlessly self-
centred it never entered his head that he could fail. And thus
when he did fail, and fail so ignominiously, he was carried away
by a rage and mortification so foamingly intense that he must
have been positively relieved when Zangiacomo, that hook-
nosed, purple-bearded fellow-German – his Italian name had

been assumed – who felt furious at the desertion of a member of his orchestra and must have held Schomberg to blame, attacked him with an hysterical violence that went far beyond the ordinary vulgar brawl. They were, according to an eye-witness, 'rolling on the floor together on this very verandah, after chasing each other all over the house, doors slamming, women screaming, seventeen of them, in the dining-room.'

This description has a touch of farce, but for Schomberg it had the hopeless ache of defeated passion. He had lost the girl – and to that Swede of all men! And it was thus, in his revengeful humour, that, terrified of 'Plain Mr. Jones' and his henchman Ricardo, he sought to kill two birds with one stone – get rid of the guests by holding out to their clutching greed and longing for excitement the bait of Samburan where, he was sure, Heyst was living on the loot stolen from Morrison. Plenty of pickings to be had there, and had easily! Rascal as Schomberg was, he could not match the cold rascality of the others, and there was some little struggle between his rage and his conscience, perhaps because the image of Lena, though now a torture, was still alluring, before he screwed himself to the pitch of confiding the plan to Ricardo. But that crafty, clear-headed 'secretary' would probably not have been enthusiastic had not Schomberg 'believed so firmly in the reality of Heyst as created by his own power of false inferences, of his hate, of his love of scandal, that he could not contain a stifled cry of conviction as sincere as most of our convictions, the disguised servants of our passions, can appear at a supreme moment.'

We know what the results of his persuasive falsehoods were – the defeat of sacrifice, the finality of separation, the death of five people – but we do not know what Schomberg thought about it all. This is of little account, no doubt, but psychologically it might have proved interesting. However, we may be certain that, though his part was probably not discovered owing to the tight-lipped loyalty of his wife (who, however, had helped Lena, out of jealousy, to escape), he soon began to bully her again and soon resumed, though perhaps not in Samarang, his favourite occupation of spreading unpleasant and damaging rumours. Fright and remorse may make a man pause in evildoing, but miraculous changes of heart seldom happen to human beings.